BETWEEN THE LINES 2

EXPLORING TEXT TYPES

Wendy Wren and Geoff Reilly

Badger Publishing

Contents

THE WILD WEST

Unit 1 — Ballads
The Duel — *Robert Service* — 4

Unit 2 — Historical Information
Western Films — *Michael Parkinson & Clyde Jeavons* — 8

Unit 3 — Text Types
Billy the Kid: Personal Recount
Billy the Kid: Film Review & Fact-file — 12

COMMUNICATION

Unit 4 — Classic Fiction
Robinson Crusoe — *Daniel Defoe* — 16

Unit 5 — Opinion
Shd skools ban txt msgs? — *Catherine Minnis* — 20
Reply — *Chris Thatcher*

Unit 6 — Advertising
Buying a Car — 24
The Chrysler PT Cruiser — *Jeff Bartlett*

WILD CHILD

Unit 7 — Modern Drama
Wolf Boy — *Peter Charlton* — 28

Unit 8 — Information Text
The Wild Boy of Aveyron — 32

Unit 9 — Case Studies/Biography
Feral Children — 36

AUSTRALIA

Unit 10 — Modern Fiction from different cultures
Walkabout — *James Vance Marshall* — 40

Unit 11 — Personal Recount (emphasis on character)
Botham on Lillee — *Ian Botham* — 44

Unit 12 — Encyclopedia – CD ROM
Great Barrier Reef — 48

EXTREME SPORTS

Unit 13 — Modern Poetry
The Ants at the Olympics — *Richard Digance* — 52

Unit 14 — Explanation
Skate History — *Joey Ferreno* — 56

Unit 15 — Personal Recount (emphasis on incidents)
Diving with Sharks — *Peter Collings* — 62

SCHOOL DAYS

Unit 16 — Classic Fiction
Jane Eyre — *Charlotte Bronte* — 68

Unit 17 — Autobiography
The Other Side of the Dale — *Gervaise Phinn* — 72

Unit 18 — Opinion
National Testing in Schools — 76

THE WILD WEST

Unit 1

The Duel

In Pat Mahooney's booze bazaar the fun was fast and free,
And Ragtime Billy spanked the baby grand;
While carolling a saucy song was Montreal Maree,
With sozzled sourdoughs giving her a hand.
When suddenly erupting in the gay and gilded hall,
A stranger draped himself upon the bar;
As in a voice like bedrock grit he hollard: "Drinks for all,"
And casually lit a long cigar.

He bore a battered stetson on the grizzle of his dome,
And a bunch of inky whiskers on his jaw;
Then suddenly I knew the guy – 'twas Black Moran from Nome,
A guinney liked greased lightning on the draw.
But no one got his number in that wild and woolly throng,
As they hailed his invitation with *eclaw*,
As they crowded round the stranger, but I knew something was wrong,
When in there stomped the Sheriff, Red McGraw.

Now Red McGraw from Arkinsaw was noted for his spunk;
He had a dozen notches on his gun;
And whether he was sober or whether he was drunk,
He kept the lousy outlaws on the run.
So now he shouts: "Say, boys, there's been a hold-up Hunker way,
And by this poke I'm throwin' on the bar,
I bet I'll get the bastard braced before another day,
Or send him where a dozen others are."

He banged the bag of gold-dust on the bar for all to see,
When in a lazy drawl the stranger spoke:
"As I'm the man you're lookin' for an' feelin' mighty free,
I reckon, Sheriff, I'll jest take yer poke.
It's pleasant meetin' you like this, an' talkin' man to man,
For all the North has heard o' Red McGraw.
I'm glad to make ye eat yer words, since I am Black Moran,
An' no man livin' beats me on the draw."

Ballads Unit 1

And as they boldly bellied, each man's hand was on his rod,
Yet at that dreaded name the Sheriff knew
A single fumbling movement and he'd go to meet his God,
The which he had no great desire to do.
So there they stood like carven wood and hushed was every breath,
We watched them glaring, staring eye to eye;
But neither drew, for either knew a second split meant death –
And so a minute...two...then three went by.

The sweat pricked on the Sheriff's brow as suddenly he broke
And limp and weak he wilted to the floor;
And then the stranger's hand shot out and grabbed the heavy poke
As jeeringly he backed up to the door.
"Say, folks," he cried, "I'm off downstream; no more of me you'll see,
But let me state the job was pretty raw....
The guy that staged the robbery he thought to pin on me
Was your bastard of a Sheriff, Red McGraw."

From Collected Verse, vol. 2 *by Robert Service*

Unit 1   The Duel

Word Work

The poem comes from a different culture – the Wild West of America – and uses vocabulary with which the reader may not be familiar.

1 Using the context in which these unfamiliar words are used, can you work out what they mean?

   Verse 1:
   a   sourdoughs
   Verse 2:
   b   stetson
   Verse 3:
   c   guinney
   Verse 4:
   d   poke
   Verse 5:
   e   rod

2 The poet also uses some unusual verbs. What do you think they mean?

   Verse 1:
   a   spanked
   b   carolling
   Verse 3:
   c   braced
   Verse 4:
   d   bellied

What is the poem about?

1 Who owned the 'booze bazaar'?
2 Who was 'the stranger'?
3 Why did the others crowd around him?
4 What do you think the notches on the Sheriff's gun signified?
5 What news had the Sheriff?
6 Why do you think he threw a bag of 'gold dust' on the bar?
7 What did the stranger challenge the Sheriff to do?
8 Why do you think the Sheriff did not shoot immediately?
9 Who backed down first?
10 What startling news did the stranger announce as he left?

Ballads Unit 1

Discussion

The Duel is written in the form of a **ballad**, a type of **narrative poetry**. Originally ballads were not written but passed by word of mouth and were a form of entertainment, often accompanied by music. They usually told stories of daring escapades and heroic figures.

A In your group, discuss and make notes on the following:
- words and phrases the poet uses to 'set the scene'
- the main events which make up the plot
- how the two main characters - Black Moran and the Sheriff - are portrayed
- the role of the narrator - how involved, or not, is he in what is going on?
- the rhyme scheme
- the rhythm
- your thoughts and opinion of the poem

B Prepare a group reading of the poem taking into consideration the roles of:
- the narrator
- Black Moran
- the Sheriff

The Author's Craft

1 What aspects of the poem would make it easy/difficult to memorise?
2 Using evidence from the poem, explain how you think the narrator feels about:
   a Black Moran
   b the Sheriff
3 What impression does the phrase 'a voice like bedrock grit' give you of Black Moran?
4 In your own words explain the meaning of:
   a 'no one got his number'
   b "make ye eat yer words"
   c "pin on me"
5 How does the poet build up the tension of the situation?
6 Explain your reaction to the ending.

Unit 2

Western Films

In 1902, two members of a notorious and audacious gang of outlaws known as The Wild Bunch came to realise that civilisation was fast closing in on the open ranges of the West and the time had come to find easier pickings elsewhere. Taking with them a pretty schoolteacher called Etta Place and $30,000 in stolen bank notes, they travelled East to New York for one last fling and then lit out for an unsuspecting South America.

The outlaws' names were Robert Leroy Parker and Harry Longbaugh – better known as Butch Cassidy and The Sundance Kid. They were virtually the last of the legendary badmen of the Western Plains – and probably the most spectacular.

The following year, with a timing which in retrospect looks marvelously apt, Edwin S. Porter made the first recognisable Western Film. It was called *The Great Train Robbery* and it became the blueprint for the countless films which, in the seventy-seven years of the cinema's history, have attempted to depict the exploits, real and imaginary, of the pioneers, frontiersmen, lawmen and bandits of the sprawling American West. It was the modest beginning of one unique mythology (the Western) building on another (the West itself), and the first visual evocation of a thrilling and epic folklore.

The Great Train Robbery was not, strictly speaking, the very first Western. A number of earlier vignettes had shown scenes of cattle round-ups and buffalo herds – even Buffalo Bill himself – and had reconstructed Western incidents already popularised and over-glamorized by the dime novel, such as hold-ups and scalpings. In 1898, W.K.L. Dickson had directed for the Edison Company a tableau called Cripple Creek Bar-room, complete with cowboys, dudes, a suspiciously masculine-looking barmaid, and a large pitcher marked 'Red Eye', and this has a stronger claim to being the first 'Western'.

But *The Great Train Robbery* was undoubtedly the first creative film drama made in America and coincidentally it happened also to be a Western. Despite its naivety and its obviously Eastern locations, it was a remarkable film for its time, employing a primitive form of editing, techniques such as the superimposition of a moving exterior scene on the 'window' of an interior set, and, at the end of the film, (or maybe at the beginning, since its function was never clearly understood and its position arbitrary) a dramatic close-up of the chief villain (George Barnes) pointing his six-gun at the audience. It also, in its ten minute length, set the classical story pattern for subsequent Westerns – crime, chase and retribution – and stamped out a number of familiar ingredients, such as the fight on top of the train and the final shoot-out.

Porter never recaptured in his later films the narrative flair which is apparent in *The Great Train Robbery*, although he directed more Westerns, including in 1907 *Rescued from an Eagle's Nest*, which is notable mainly for having D.W. Griffiths in the leading role. But *The Great Train Robbery* was a big commercial success as well as a cinematic milestone, and it inspired a rash of imitations sufficient to set the genre well and truly in motion.

Historical Information — Unit 2

Train robberies were still a fact of life in the first decade of the century, so this theme retained its popularity; but other formulas began to develop also, most importantly a trend away from groups of goodies and baddies towards the individual heroes and villains. Another Edison film of 1906, *A Race for Millions*, went so far as to conclude with a gun-duel on the main street (most of which was a very obvious painted set).

This trend was leading inevitably up to the one major ingredient which was so far lacking in the Western – the star-hero. Audiences needed a central character on which to concentrate their attention, and he suddenly transpired in 1908 in the stocky person of G.M. Anderson (right), soon to be known almost exclusively as Broncho Billy. Anderson's rise to stardom was almost accidental. He had talked his way into a small part in *The Great Train Robbery* and then set about learning the movie business as both actor and director. He formed with George K. Spoor what was to become one of the most distinguished of the early movie studios – Essanay – and made one significant move by setting up a West Coast studio in California, close to the authentic geography which was swiftly to become an obvious vital part of Western film-making. (Although as late as 1915 Edison were still using Eastern locations – as exposed most embarrassingly in *The Corporal's Daughter* which, in the scene showing the cavalry riding out of a fort, carelessly allows a modern main road, complete with drain, to slip into the frame.)

Anderson recognised the need for an identifiable cowboy hero, but he had no intention at first of casting himself in the part – a step he was, however, forced to take when he could find no one else available for the lead in a short Western called *Broncho Billy and the Baby*.

The film was a remarkable success, audiences taking readily to the Broncho Billy character: the courageous, basically decent good-badman prepared to sacrifice his freedom to help a child in distress. They liked also (and, before the glamorised star-system, were more ready to accept) the air of reality which Broncho Billy got from Anderson's rugged, plain, amiable, bulky and boyish gauche appearance.

In seven years Billy appeared in something approaching five hundred one- and two-reelers, sticking to the noble, faintly tragic lone-rider characterisation with which he began the series.

From A Pictorial History of Westerns *by Michael Parkinson and Clyde Jeavons*

Unit 2 Western Films

Word Work

1 Find the adjectives in the passage which are made from the following nouns. Using a dictionary and the context of the passage, explain the meaning of each adjective.

- a notoriety
- b audacity
- c legend
- d marvel
- e suspicion
- f coincidence
- g cinema
- h authenticity
- i identity
- j courage
- k glamour
- l tragedy

2 Writing about certain topics often includes specialised vocabulary. All these words are connected with film-making and the cinema. What do they mean?

- a vignettes
- b directed
- c tableau
- d locations
- e role
- f reelers

What is the passage about?

1 What were Robert Leroy Parker and Harry Longbaugh also known as?
2 In what year did Porter make 'the first recognisable Western film'?
3 What was it called?
4 The exploits of which four groups of people do Westerns attempt to depict?
5 What 'classical story pattern' did this film set up?
6 What followed the trend of having 'groups of goodies and baddies'?
7 Who was the first 'star-hero'?
8 What was the advantage of Essanay setting up a West Coast studio?
9 What was the first film in which Anderson took a leading role?
10 Approximately how many films did he make as Broncho Billy?

Historical Information   Unit 2

Discussion

> *Western Films* is an **information text** dealing with the historical background of the genre. In it the writers trace the rise in popularity of the Western film from very humble beginnings.

A In your group, discuss and make notes on the following:
- the writers' intentions – purpose
- the writers' attitude to their subject
- the intended audience
- the paragraph structure:
  - How many paragraphs?
  - What is each one about?
- the effect of the opening paragraph
- the use of words and phrases which help the reader to understand the main ingredients in these early westerns

B Discuss the Western film genre. Make a list of reasons why it is very popular with some people whilst it has little or no appeal for others.

The Author's Craft

1. What impression are the writers trying to create by using such words as 'imaginary', 'mythology' and 'folklore' to describe the contents of Westerns?
2. Explain in your own words:
   a 'over-glamorised'
   b 'cinematic milestone'
   c 'rash of imitations'
3. How do the writers give the impression that 'location' was an important element in these early films?
4. What reasons do the writers give for the arrival of the 'star-hero' in Westerns?
5. From details in the passage, does Broncho Billy fit our modern idea of a film star? Why? Why not?
6. What impression of the Broncho Billy character do the writers wish to convey by calling him a 'good-badman'?

Unit 3

Billy the Kid

Passage A: Personal Recount

My father and mother moved to Lincoln New Mexico in 1863, when I was about nine years old. I do not remember very much about the trip but we moved in a wagon with an ox team. My father settled on a place about a quarter of a mile east of Lincoln and farmed. He used oxen altogether on the farm.

I can remember when we lived in Manzano that the oxen had big horns and the ropes were fastened to their horns, but when we moved to Lincoln they used yokes on the oxen. I had never seen them before. When we planted corn at Lincoln my father drove the team of oxen and I dropped the corn in the furrow.

Father would go up in the mountains near our house and cut down trees for wood and would put a chain around the tree and the oxen would snake the tree down the mountain side to the house. When I was about eighteen years old I went to work for the McSween's. I stayed with them for about two years. I remember that one winter Billy the Kid stayed with the McSween's for about seven months. I guess he boarded with them. He was an awfully nice young fellow with light brown hair, blue eyes, and rather big front teeth. He always dressed very neatly.

He used to practice target shooting a lot. He would throw up a can and would twirl his six gun on his finger and he could hit the can six times before it hit the ground. He rode a big roan horse about ten or twelve hands high, all that winter and when this horse was out in the pasture Billy would go to the gate and whistle and the horse would come up to the gate to him. That horse would follow Billy and mind him like a dog. He was a very fast horse and could out run most of the other horses around there. I never went out with Billy but once.

Captain Baca was sheriff then and once some tough outlaws came to Lincoln and rode up and down the streets and shot out window lights in the houses and terrorized people. Captain Baca told Billy the Kid to take some men and go after these men. Billy took me and Florencio and Jose Chaves and Santano Mayes with him. The outlaws went to the upper Ruidoso and we followed them. We caught up with them and shot it out with them. One of the outlaws was killed and the other ran away. None of us were hurt.

When the Lincoln County war broke out my father did not want to get into it so he made me quit working for the McSween's and come home and stay there. My father did not take any part in the war. I was married to Crecencia Sales in 1881 at Lincoln. We never had any children of our own but we adopted two girls. One is married and the other lives with me now at Lincoln. My wife died about ten years ago. My father and mother both died at Lincoln and are buried there.

I still live on the old place that my father settled on so many years ago. I have been Justice of the Peace of Lincoln County for about twenty years at different times and was Probate Judge from about 1900 to 1904. I got so old that I would not serve as Justice of the Peace any more.

I have lived all of my life in New Mexico and have been in Lincoln County for seventy-five years.

From the WPA Files of the Library of Congress
(Scribe's tribute to Billy the Kid – www.geocities.com/SouthBeach/Marina/2057/Billy_the_Kid.html)

Passage B: Film Review
Billy the Kid USA (1989)
Colour, Available on videocassette
Cast:
Governor Lew Wallace ~ Wilford Brimley
Celsa ~ Julie Carmen
William Bonney ~ Val Kilmer
Pat Garrett ~ Duncan Regehr
Directed by: William A. Graham
Screenplay by: Gore Vidal

Review
Gore Vidal's Billy the Kid (Turner Home Entertainment) is what some might refer to as a romanticized version of Billy's tale. I, for one, believe that Vidal did some fantasizing, too. After all, Billy the Kid/William Bonney is known for being a really miserable punk, who shot people in the back, rustled cattle and stole horses. Historically speaking, even criminals like Jesse James had no good word for this Billy the Kid character. Nineteen or not, he was unspeakably bad!

However, if you enjoy Westerns, you'll more than likely like this one. The cinematography was outstanding and the story-line is okay, if you can swallow Billy the Kid (Val Kilmer, inset) as a caring and nice guy. Gore Vidal would like us to believe that poor Billy was 'so' misunderstood in history prior to this film.

This review written by NightMare. (www.planetkilmer.com/btk.htm)

Passage C: Fact-file
Born: November 23, 1859/60, New York, USA
Died: July 14, 1881, Fort Sunmer, New Mexico
As a child went by the name Henry McCarty. At his trial he used the name William H. Bonney. Scholars are divided as to which was his true name.

Reputed to have killed at least 27 men before being gunned down by Sheriff Pat Garrett.

Born in New York he moved with his parents to Kansas where his father died. They then moved to Colorado where his mother remarried. In his early teens the family moved to New Mexico where Billy began a life of lawlessness. In December 1880 he was captured by Pat Garrett and stood trial for murder. In April 1881 he was found guilty and sentenced to hang but he escaped, killing two deputies in the process. Garrett tracked him down and killed him on the evening of July 14, 1881. His grave is in Fort Sumner, New Mexico.

Scholarly opinion about Billy the Kid is divided. Some believe that he was, in fact, Ollie L. 'Brushy Bill' Roberts who escaped from jail, lived in Mexico, rode in Wild West shows and died in 1950 in Hico, Texas.

Unit 3   Billy the Kid

Word Work

1 Plural means more than one. These plurals are used in the passages.
   Write them as singular. Check in a dictionary.
   - a oxen
   - b teeth
   - c people
   - d men
   - e children
   - f deputies

2 The following words do not make their past tense by adding 'ed'.
   Write the past tense of each. Check your answers by finding the past tense words in the passages.
   - a drive
   - b go
   - c ride
   - d come
   - e shoot
   - f tell
   - g take
   - h catch
   - i break
   - j make
   - k steal
   - l stand

What are the passages about?

Passage A
1 Where did the writer move to in 1863?
2 Where was he living when he met Billy the Kid?
3 On what occasion did the writer ride out with Billy the Kid?
4 What happened at the shoot out?

Passage B
5 Who plays Billy the Kid in the film?
6 In what way is Gore Vidal involved in the film?
7 What, according to the writer, is the one outstanding feature of the film?

Passage C
8 What other names is it thought Billy the Kid may have used?
9 List the places Billy lived from his birth to his death.
10 On what date did he stand trial for murder?

Discussion

The three non fiction passages about Billy the Kid are different **text types**. Each has a different style, is written for a different purpose and will most probably appeal to a different audience.

14

Text Types   Unit 3

In groups, discuss and make notes on the following:

For each passage decide:
- the text type
- the writer's purpose
- the intended audience

Passage A

Find details in the passage which gives the reader information about:
- Billy's physical appearance
- his personality
- the writer's attitude towards him

Passage B

Find details in the passage which:
- give the reader information about Billy's personality
- show the writer's attitude to the film

Passage C

Highlight the words and phrases in the passage that show much of what is known about Billy the Kid is educated guesswork.

The Author's Craft

Passage A

1 What impression do you get of the writer's relationship with Billy the Kid?
2 In what ways does the writer's description of Billy's character:
   a agree with the information in Passage B?
   b contradict the information in Passage B?

Passage B

3 Explain what the writer means when she says 'I, for one, believe that Vidal did some fantasising, too'.
4 How does the writer's view of Billy the Kid differ from Gore Vidal's?

Passage C

5 Find and copy an example of:
   a factual information   b opinion
6 In terms of the writer's attitude to Billy the Kid, how is this passage different from Passage A and Passage B?
7 Based on what you have read, say whether you think Billy the Kid was a hero or a villain. Explain your reasons.

COMMUNICATION

Unit 4

Robinson Crusoe

This was the pleasantest year of all the life I led in this place. Friday began to talk pretty well, and understand the names of almost everything I had occasion to call for, and of every place I had to send him to, and talk a great deal to me; so that, in short, I began now to have some use for my tongue again, which, indeed, I had very little occasion for before, that is to say, about speech. Besides the pleasure of talking to him, I had a singular satisfaction in the fellow himself. His simple, unfeigned honesty appeared to me more and more every day, and I began really to love the creature; and, on his side, I believe he loved me more than it was possible for him ever to love anything before.

    I had a mind once to try if he had any hankering inclination to his own country again; and having learned him English so well that he could answer me almost any questions, I asked him whether the nation that he belonged to never conquered in battle? At which he smiled, and said, "Yes, yes, we always fight the better;" that is, he meant, always get the better in fight; and so we began the following discourse: "You always fight the better," said I. "How came you to be taken prisoner then, Friday?"

Friday. – My nation beat much for all that.

Master. – How beat? If your nation beat them, how came you to be taken?

Friday. – They more many than my nation in the place where me was; they take one, two, three, and me. My nation overbeat them in the yonder place, where me no was; there my nation take one, two, great thousand.

Master. – But why did not your side recover you from the hands of your enemies, then?

Friday. – They run one, two, three, and me, and make go in the canoe; my nation have no canoe that time.

Master. – Well, Friday, and what does your nation do with the men they take? Do they carry them away and eat them, as these did?

Friday. – Yes, my nation eat mans too; eat all up.

Master. – Where do they carry them?
Friday. – Go to other place, where they think.
Master. – Do they come hither?
Friday. – Yes, yes, they come hither; come other else place.
Master. – Have you been here with them?
Friday. – Yes, I been here. (Points to the NW. side of the island, which, it seems, was their side.)

By this I understood that my man Friday had formerly been among the savages who used to come on shore on the farther part of the island, on the same man-eating occasions that he was now brought for; and, some time after, when I took the courage to carry him to that side, being the same I formerly mentioned, he presently knew the place, and told me he was there once when they eat up twenty men, two women, and one child. He could not tell twenty in English, but he numbered them by laying so many stones on a row, and pointing to me to tell them over.

From Robinson Crusoe *by Daniel Defoe*

Unit 4   Robinson Crusoe

Word Work

1 Explain the meaning of the following words as they are used in the passage:

   Paragraph 1
   a tongue
   b singular
   c unfeigned

   Paragraph 2
   d hankering
   e inclination
   f discourse

2 Find expressions in the passage which mean:
   a They outnumbered my tribe where I was fighting.
   b My tribe captured many enemies.
   c My tribe did not have their canoes with them and were unable to rescue me.

What is the passage about?

1 Who is Friday?
2 What does Robinson Crusoe like about Friday?
3 Which quotation shows that Robinson Crusoe taught Friday English?
4 What does Friday mean when he says, "My nation beat much for all that"?
5 Where do Friday's tribe take their prisoners, when they capture them in battle?
6 What does Friday's tribe do with its captives?
7 How did Friday show Robinson Crusoe the number of prisoners that had been brought to the island by his tribe?
8 How many prisoners had Friday's tribe brought to Robinson Crusoe's island?
9 Which phrases or expressions show that Robinson Crusoe was anxious about taking Friday to the north-west side of the island?

Classic Fiction Unit 4

💬 Discussion

> *Robinson Crusoe* is an example of **classic fiction**. It was written by Daniel Defoe in 1719. A fictional tale of a shipwrecked sailor, it was based on the adventures of a seaman, Alexander Selkirk, who had been marooned on one of the Juan Fernández Islands off the coast of Chile. The **novel**, full of detail about Crusoe's ingenious attempts to overcome the hardships of the island, has become one of the classics of English literature.

A In your groups, discuss and make notes on the following:
- what impression you gain of:
  – Robinson Crusoe
  – Friday
- Crusoe's attitude to Friday
- any other stories about surviving on an uninhabited island
- why writers would choose to base stories on lone survivors on desert islands
- the immediate problems of surviving on an uninhabited island

B Imagine that you are a castaway on a desert island but, mysteriously, a trunk is washed up with you. It contains various possessions that will make your stay on the island more bearable, even though they are of no practical use in helping you to escape:
- Which eight pieces of music would be included?
- Which three books would be in the trunk?
- Which three favourite possessions would be in the trunk?

💡 The Author's Craft

1. In your own words, explain how the writer conveys to the reader that Friday does not speak English as his mother tongue?
2. Which words, phrases or expressions show that the text was written a long time ago?
3. From evidence in the text, what impression does the dialogue create of the relationship between Robinson Crusoe and Friday?
4. What signs are there in the passage that Robinson Crusoe feels that he is superior to Friday?

Unit 5

Shd skools ban txt msgs?

English teacher Catherine Minnis says text messaging can damage children's use of English.

Although I have no objection to children owning mobile phones, as a teacher of English I do object to text messaging because its etiquette is now creeping into my pupils' exercise books.

At first, I thought they were either being ironic or just plain cheeky, but after questioning some of my middle-set Year 8s, I realised that some of them actually believe that 'b4' and '2day' are correct spellings and that 'ru' is an acceptable substitute for 'are you?'.

For one who has spent years trying to eliminate 'alot', 'aswell' and 'infact', these text abbreviations represent the proverbial last straw.

It isn't just spelling that is affected: in text messaging, punctuation doesn't exist, unless it's part of a symbol, such as ':-~)' meaning, 'I have a cold' (turn it sideways!). Capital letters aren't used either, unless in the middle of a word!

Those who laugh at my pedantry and concern are welcome to view my lower school-books. Watch me add in all that missing punctuation, and see all those misplaced or missing capitals. All the good that the literacy hour has done is being undone, in many cases, by text messaging.

Adults have a chance of being able to distinguish between Standard English and text slang, and hopefully will use each according to audience and purpose, but my fear is that children will grow up never appreciating the difference.

Ironically, some of my Year 7 pupils, who cannot be persuaded to part with 50p to buy a second-hand dictionary to improve their spelling, will happily fork out a couple of pounds for a text messaging dictionary. Undoubtedly, these wacky acronyms and emoticons (icons used to express emotions in messaging) are part of a very clever new system and clearly much thought has gone into it. Like any language, there are rules and conventions. For example, most vowels are missed out and capital letters stand in place of doubled consonants.

However, since speed is its very essence, stock abbreviations and phrases (if you can call them that!) are used and I feel that they limit a child's vocabulary. I'm convinced that text messaging is not going to help our children express themselves in quite the same way that the rich and varied English language can. I believe schools need to take action to limit the damage messaging can do and to send a clear message to pupils about what is and is not acceptable English usage.

So U dnt thnk txt msgng shud B used in skuls?

It stimulates an interest in communicating, says Head Chris Thatcher.

Every generation has its own sub-culture and the youngsters in our schools now are no different. It would be a mistake not to recognise what is happening in their world and to tap into the enthusiasm that text messaging has for them. But more than that, text messaging is fast becoming a recognised and developing means of communication with many business applications. Three billion text messages are expected to be sent this year – many of those cannot be attributed to a teenage craze.

Can we afford to ignore that – either as a facet of teenage life or as a potentially powerful element of adult communication?

We should try to understand why it has become so important to the young people of today. It is, firstly, private and non-intrusive. No one but the recipient knows that they have received a message. Secondly it is fast and relatively easy to send – far less hassle than even the simple e-mail and it doesn't require long periods connected to the internet through either a computer or a WAP phone. Thirdly, the brief nature of most text messages forces the users to look for shortcuts and this has created a whole new vocabulary that is quite often hard for adults not used to text messaging to understand. That in itself is a very positive advantage – to youngsters, anything that cuts adults out and creates a new private world for them, is appealing.

Communication of any sort between youngsters has to be valued and text messaging, with its totally new approach, is simply another mechanism for communication to take place.

So our dilemma is do we discourage it (or even try to ban it) thus pushing it underground and making it, in a sense, even more appealing. Or do we use it as an opportunity to extend creativity and build it into our teaching.

I really do believe that the latter approach will have a two-fold effect. Firstly it will recognise and use a mechanism already popular with many youngsters and will bring with it a great degree of enthusiasm. Secondly, it will, so to speak, bring it out of the closet and effectively remove it from the secret world it currently inhabits.

I would be very surprised if there aren't already in existence teaching programmes where imaginative teachers are actively working to find new and creative ways to use text messaging in their lessons. When I was at college we were taught to incorporate many different styles of writing into our teaching. Helping youngsters to appreciate the intended audience for their creations changed the style and mechanism that was used to construct the work.

Yes, text messaging used indiscriminately can get in the way of teachers delivering the curriculum. The real answer is not to ban it but to help pupils to use it selectively and wisely – surely part of the function of any school with a wide variety of communication mechanisms.

And before you ask, yes I use it. I find it saves time, effort and enables me to get quick answers. Confining yourself to 160 characters is almost an art form in itself! It's quick, and unlike a phone call, doesn't intrude. Over 2 U!

Unit 5   Shd Skools ban txt msgs?
So U dnt think txt msgng shud B used in skuls?

Word Work

1 Explain the meaning of the following words as they are used in the passage:

Passage A
- a etiquette
- b ironic
- c substitute
- d eliminate
- e proverbial
- f pedantry
- g slang
- h conventions

Passage B
- i generation
- j sub-culture
- k facet
- l non-intrusive
- m recipient
- n vocabulary
- o mechanism
- p dilemma

2 The authors use a number of unusual expressions. Use the context of the passages to work out what the following mean:

Passage A
- a 'the proverbial last straw'
- b 'will happily fork out'
- c 'wacky acronyms and emoticons'
- d 'stock abbreviations and phrases'

Passage B
- e 'to tap into the enthusiasm'
- f 'cannot be attributed to a teenage craze'
- g 'far less hassle'
- h 'that cuts adults out'
- i 'pushing it underground'
- j 'bring it out of the closet'

What are the passages about?

Passage A

1 Why do you think the writer believes that text messaging damages children's use of English?
2 Why do you think the writer 'has spent years trying to eliminate "alot", "aswell" and "infact"'?
3 Why is the writer worried about punctuation?
4 What problems are caused by the use or misuse of capital letters?
5 Which conventions of text messaging does the writer give as examples?

Passage B

6 How many text messages does the writer suggest will be sent this year?
7 What three reasons are given for the importance of text messaging for young people?
8 What dilemma for teachers does the writer outline?
9 What are the two effects that could arise from building text messaging into teaching?
10 What limit is placed on the number of characters used in a text message?

Discussion

The above passages are examples of modern, non-fiction writing, in the form of **persuasive magazine articles**. In the passages, two teachers explain how text messaging is either a problem or an opportunity for teachers, in the development of communication skills.

A In your groups, discuss and make notes on the following:
- The impressions that you gain of the attitudes of the teachers in the passages to the development of communication skills.
- The advantages and disadvantages of text messaging, compared with accuracy in the use of spelling, punctuation and grammar.
- In what ways does the use of acronyms, abbreviations and emoticons improve communication or hinder it?
- The strengths and weaknesses of the arguments of the teachers in the two passages. Which arguments are the most convincing?
- Has the writer of Passage A or Passage B succeeded in convincing you to adopt their views on text messaging? Discuss and explain your reasons.

B In Passage A, the teacher explains some of the conventions of text messaging.
- Compile a list of the rules and conventions of text messaging for your group.

The Author's Craft

1. Text messaging is not written in full, grammatically correct, Standard English sentences. What effect does this have?
2. In the first passage, the writer gives information about text messaging. Find two examples of such information.
3. What major argument does the writer of Passage A put forward for banning text messaging? Explain your reasons for finding her argument convincing or unconvincing.
4. In Passage B, what are the writer's arguments for encouraging text messages? Explain your reasons for finding his arguments convincing or unconvincing.
5. In April 2001, the *Guardian* newspaper introduced the first UK text messaging poetry competition. There were 7,500 poems entered for the competition. The winning poem, inspired by her grandmother, was written by a 22 year old student. Write your own text message poem, inspired by a friend or relative.

Unit 6

Buying a Car

DELBOY'S MOTORS

97 P HONDA PRELUDE 2.0i AUTOMATIC SPORTS COUPE
(NEW SHAPE) in velvet blue metallic, PAS, air con, alloys, sunroof, 1 former **£5990**

97 X VAUXHALL VECTRA 2.0i GLS 16V HATCHBACK
5 door, in velvet blue metallic, PAS, air bag, air con, stereo, low mileage, well maintained **£3990**

97 P SCORPIO ULTIMA 2.3 16V AUTOMATIC EXEC SALOON brilliant silver, raven leather,
PAS, air con, parksonic top spec., good mileage, 1 local owner FSH **£5999**

96 P MITSUBISHI CARISMA 1.6 GLXi HATCHBACK 5 door in inferno red,
PAS, air bag, sunroof, stereo, elec. windows, central locking, a genuine 40,000 miles, only.... **£3999**

95 N VOLVO 440 1.9 Tdi TURBO DIESEL HATCHBACK 5 door, in inferno red,
grey velour interior, PAS, airbags, elec. sunroof, windows, mirrors, stereo, local car **£2999**

94 M VAUXHALL CORSA 1.4 Lsi HATCHBACK
3 door, turqoise, grey trim, 2 owners, good mileage, low tax & insurance, superb **£2699**

www.delboys-motors.com Apply on-line to obtain finance details

CLASSIC QUALITY MOTORS

~ Where do you want to drive today? ~

98 S BMW Z3 2.8i ROADSTER
alpine white, black lthr, hard-top, roll-over bars, 26k **£18,995**

99 T BMW Z3 1.9i
atlanta blue, anth cloth, black hood, elipslid alloys 26k **£16,495**

01 Y BMW 330Ci AUTO SPORT
orient blue, lt beige lthr, sports model, CD, 10k **£30,995**

97 R BMW 520i AUTO SE TOURER
montreal blue, marine blue cloth, wood trim 67k **£11,995**

98 R BMW 540i AUTO
arctic silver, grey lthr, sat nav, BMW bodykit, 40k **£23,995**

01 Y BMW 728i AUTO SALOON
anthracite, black lthr, M sports pack, comms pack 7k **£36,995**

Sales, service, parts, MOT, tuning, all makes
T: 01744 128813   F: 01744 128814   e-mail: delboy@motors.com

Advertising   Unit 6

The Chrysler PT Cruiser at the SEMA show

No question, the Chrysler PT Cruiser dominated the 2001 SEMA show in Las Vegas, where dozens of companies used the retro car to showcase their aftermarket components. While our show coverage featured several PT Cruisers on the show floor, we've compiled a look at several standout vehicles photographed outside in more natural settings. As you can see, the possibilities with this distinctive, award-winning car are limited only by imagination and budget.

by Jeff Bartlett
http://www.motortrend.com/dec00/pt/1.html

Unit 6 Buying a Car
The Chrysler PT Cruiser at the SEMA show

Word Work

1 Explain the meaning of the following abbreviations as they are used in Passage A:
   a PAS
   b Air con
   c Spec.
   d FSH
   e Elec.
   f Lthr
   g Lt. beige
   h CD
   i 10k
   j sat nav

2 The author of Passage B uses a number of unusual expressions. Use the context of the passage to work out what the following mean:
   a 'No question'
   b 'retro car'
   c 'to showcase'
   d 'aftermarket components'
   e 'standout vehicles'

What are the passages about?

Passage A

1 What are the main features of cars that are highlighted in advertisements?
2 Why does the advertiser break up the advertisements with 'banners'?
3 What services are offered to customers by Delboy's Motors?
4 What are the different ways that customers can use to contact Delboy's Motors?
5 What do you think that Delboy's Motors means by the motto 'Where do you want to drive today?'?

Passage B

6 Which car was the most impressive at the 2001 SEMA show?
7 What use did companies make of the 2001 SEMA show?
8 Why did the publicity material photograph several PT Cruisers outside the show?
9 The publicity material uses a number of words and phrases to promote the qualities of the car shown in the photograph. Explain what the following words and phrases suggest about this car:
   a modified
   b retro
   c distinctive
   d award-winning

Advertising   Unit 6

Discussion

> The above passages are examples of **modern, non-fiction writing to inform**, with strong graphical elements, in the form of advertisements or publicity materials. In the texts, language is often abbreviated, layout is modified and graphics are used to highlight the subjects.

A In your groups, discuss and make notes on the following:
- the different use of images in Passage A and Passage B
- the advantages and disadvantages of using abbreviations
- the effects on different 'audiences' of using abbreviations and technical terms
- the use of persuasive language
- the strengths and weaknesses of the different layouts used in Passages A and B

Compare the two passages and decide which is most helpful to the reader in communicating its purpose.

B If you could choose any car to own, what would it be? What would this tell us about your character?

The Author's Craft

1 Car advertisements are not written in full, grammatically correct, Standard English sentences. Does this help or hinder the reader in understanding their information?
2 In Passage A, the advertisement abbreviations are used to reduce the costs of paying for the advertisement. Are the abbreviations likely to be understood more easily by any particular groups of readers?
3 Writing to inform is usually characterised by clear layout, and precise and straightforward explanation appropriate to the target audience. To what extent is this true of the passages above?
4 Some advertising companies believe that owners choose cars that reflect their personalities. What kind of character do you think would drive the car in the photograph accompanying Passage B?
5 Has the writer of Passage A or Passage B been the most successful in fulfilling their purpose for the target audience? Give your reasons for your opinion and point out examples to support your views.

WILD CHILD

Unit 7

Wolf Boy

(The WOLF BOY is pulled back onto the table and all three crowd around to examine him.)

	CHORUS 1	Definitely a human boy-child.
	CHORUS 2	No clothes. Disgraceful!
	CHORUS 3	Covered in scars.
	CHORUS 1	Ten or eleven years old.
5	CHORUS 2	Runs on all fours.
	CHORUS 3	Makes animal sounds. Can't speak.
	CHORUS 1	Or can't hear. Maybe we need to test further. (Speaking slowly and carefully) What is your name? (No response)
10	CHORUS 2	Where do you come from?
	CHORUS 3	Who are your parents?
	CHORUS 1	How many fingers?
	CHORUS 2	What colour is my tie?
	CHORUS 3	Where is the window? (Their questions become louder and more frantic.)
15	CHORUS 1	Two plus two?
	CHORUS 2	Spell cat.
	CHORUS 3	What is the capital of France?
	CHORUS 1	How many days in a week?
	CHORUS 2	What time is it?
20	CHORUS 3	What is the…?
	CHORUS 1	Where is the…?
	CHORUS 2	How can we…?
	CHORUS 3	Where?
	CHORUS 1	When?
25	CHORUS 2	Who?
	CHORUS 3	How?

28

CHORUS 1, 2 & 3   Why?

(As soon as they stop, the WOLF BOY begins to laugh. Softly at first, then growing into beautiful, innocent laughter. His face remains blank, showing no emotion or expression. The CHORUS look on aghast. The WOLF BOY stops and sits silently, staring straight ahead.)

CHORUS 1	It is obvious, gentlemen, that the child is an idiot. Doesn't understand a thing. Deaf. Dumb. And stupid.
CHORUS 2	It is obvious, gentlemen, that the child was left in the forest by his parents because he was an idiot. They left him to die, but somehow he survived and lived with the animals – wolves.
CHORUS 3	It is obvious, gentlemen, that an idiot could not survive alone in the forest. We have just had the coldest winter since ninety five. The child must have some sense in order to live for probably years in the forest. He just seems like an idiot because he's forgotten how to behave like a human.
CHORUS 1	Maybe you're right. I don't know.
CHORUS 2	I think he's an idiot. It's plain for all to see.
CHORUS 3	Well, if we can't agree, then we must do the correct thing.
CHORUS 1	Yes, yes. The correct thing.
CHORUS 2	It must be done.
CHORUS 3	We must take him to an expert.
CHORUS 1, 2 & 3	A genius, a specialist, a star. Someone who knows more than us by far! But who do we turn to, where do we go To find the right person, who's certain to know? A doctor? A lawyer? A scientist? A priest? Just how many people are experts on beasts?

From Wolf Boy *by Peter Charlton*

Unit 7   Wolf Boy

Word Work

1 Explain the meaning of the following words as they are used in the play script:
   a disgraceful
   b (stage direction) frantic
   c aghast
   d idiot
   e dumb
   f human

2 Find expressions in the passage which mean:
   a a person with extraordinary imaginative, creative or intellectual abilities
   b an actor or actress who attracts the biggest audiences
   c a member of the legal profession
   d a minister of the church

What is the passage about?

1 What was disgraceful about the boy when he was found?
2 What was the condition of the boy's body when he was found?
3 How old do they think the boy is?
4 What was unusual about the way the boy moved?
5 When the boy does not respond to their questions, what do the questioners conclude?
6 Why do some questioners think the boy was left in the forest?
7 What reasons are given as to why the boy cannot be considered an idiot?
8 In what year was the last severe winter?
9 What is the correct thing that the questioners decide to do?
10 Who do the questioners think are the right people to ask for help?

Modern Drama   Unit 7

💬 Discussion

> The extract from *Wolf Boy* is an example of **modern fiction**, in the form of a **play script**. In the extract, a boy has been found living wild with wolves, in the forests near Aveyron, in France. The play script explores what so-called civilised societies judge to be human.

A In your groups, discuss and make notes on the following:
- the impressions that you gain of the Chorus
- the contrast between the quiet innocence of the Wolf Boy's silence and the constant questions from the Chorus
- the vocabulary used by the Chorus to describe the Wolf Boy
- how the writer builds up the tension of the situation
- the relationships between Chorus 1, Chorus 2 and Chorus 3
- the meaning and effectiveness of the final question

B What do you think the audience learns from the Wolf Boy about the qualities of being human? Do you think that the Chorus act in a civilised way towards the Wolf Boy? Discuss and explain your reasons.

💡 The Author's Craft

1. The first seven lines of the scene are not written in full, grammatically correct sentences. What effect does this have?
2. What do you think the questions on lines 10-18 would reveal to us about the Wolf Boy? Why did the writer include these particular questions for the Chorus?
3. What effect do the questions on lines 19-27 have on the rhythm and mood of the scene? Why do you think the writer used this technique?
4. Why has the writer included a detailed stage direction half-way through the scene? If the actors followed the direction, what effect do you think it was intended to produce?
5. In lines 32-45 the writer repeatedly uses the word 'idiot'. Why is the word used so often and what impression is it intended to create of the Wolf Boy and of the Chorus?
6. In the final nine lines, the writer has used some rhyme. Why do you think he has done so? What effect does it have on the scene?

31

… Unit 8

Wild Boy of Aveyron

A wild boy was captured in the forest near Lacaune, France, in 1797. The boy was dragged by his captors, kicking and struggling, to be put on show in the square. The wild boy managed to escape, but in 1798 he was recaptured by three hunters as he was climbing a tree. He was then taken to the house of a widow, who fed and clothed him for a week. Yet, the boy escaped, once again. However, the wild boy was now less cautious of human company, and began to visit farms looking for food.

In 1800, with winter at its worst, the hungry wild boy wandered near a village called Saint Sernin, where he was captured again, this time by a local tanner named Vidal. After that, the boy came to be known as Victor and he never returned to the wild.

In 1799, Jean-Marc Gaspard Itard heard reports of a boy abandoned in the woods near Aveyron, France, who had apparently been raised by wolves. 'Victor, the Wild Boy of Aveyron,' as he had come to be called, was chosen by Itard as an experimental subject. Itard wanted to prove the 'blank slate' theory: that a person could become, or be made into, whatever one wants. Itard had the child brought to Paris and entrusted to the care of his housekeeper. Victor was probably in his early teens, a child with severe mental retardation who likely had been abandoned by his parents.

Napoleon's brother, Lucien Bonaparte, who was the Minister for the Interior, demanded that the boy had to be examined by experts. Victor was exhibited in a cage, where he would rock back and forth and appear completely apathetic. The pioneer psychologist, Philippe Pinel, examined the boy and diagnosed him as an incurable idiot. Pinel did not believe the story of Victor's wild origins.

Itard saw Victor as someone who had not been tainted by civilisation, and who could become the perfect human being. The 'blank slate' would be filled with carefully selected information. From a child who could not speak, would not sleep in a bed, wear clothes or eat cooked food, Victor made tremendous progress. He learned to use simple ways of communicating and interacting with others, particularly Itard's housekeeper.

As time passed, Itard grew frustrated, not seeing the great gains he hoped for, and gave up his hope of Victor becoming able to live a normal life. Living outside of civilisation had not protected Victor from corruption, as Itard had thought; it had only deprived him of language, understanding and human affection. Even with his limited success, Itard did prove that children with mental retardation could improve to some extent. This was to have a positive influence on many of the educators of the following century.

In 1798, the same year that Victor was captured, Thomas Malthus (1766-1834), a British clergyman and economist, published his 'Essay on the Principle of Population'. He argued that the rapidly-increasing population would soon outstrip their food supply. If this happened, there would be widespread famine and mass starvation. He argued for cutting the birth rate and advocated that anybody 'defective', who looked or behaved differently from the rest of society, should be eliminated. If Malthus had his way, Victor would have been one of those eliminated. Thus, only those who are 'normal', those who can make the greatest contribution to society, would survive.

After Monsieur Itard had completed his research, Victor went to stay with a local widow called Madame Guerin. He lived quietly with Madame Guerin until his death in 1828.

From www.occultopedia.com/w/wild_boy_aveyron.htm

Unit 8 Wild Boy of Aveyron

Word Work

1 Explain the meaning of the following words as they are used in the passage:

Paragraph 1
a widow
b cautious

Paragraph 2
c tanner

Paragraph 3
d experimental
e theory
f retardation

Paragraph 4
g apathetic
h pioneer

Paragraph 5
i tainted

Paragraph 6
j corruption

Paragraph 7
k clergyman
l economist
m defective

2 Find expressions in the passage which mean:
a removed, got rid of
b extreme lack of food, starvation
c scientific study of a subject
d argued for, spoke up for

What is the passage about?

1 What was the name given to the wild boy?
2 Where was the wild boy first captured?
3 In which year was the boy first captured?
4 In which year was he captured for the last time?
5 Who was the person that finally captured the wild boy?
6 Who was the scientist who wanted to use the wild boy for experiments?
7 What position was held by Napoleon's brother?
8 Who published his 'Essay on the Principle of Population' in 1798?
9 Where did the wild boy live when the experiments were finished?
10 With whom did the wild boy live until his death?

Information Text   Unit 8

Discussion

Wild Boy of Aveyron is an example of **non-fiction writing to inform**. In the passage, a boy has been found living wild with wolves, in the forests near Aveyron, in France. The passage explores what happened to the boy, after he was captured.

A In your groups, discuss and make notes on the following:
- the impressions that you gain of the wild boy
- the attitude of Jean-Marc Gaspard Itard to the wild boy
- the attitude of Philippe Pinel to the wild boy and Itard's research
- how successful Itard was in proving the 'blank slate' theory
- the theories of Thomas Malthus
- what would be considered defective and normal today

B What do you think the reader learns from *Wild Boy of Aveyron* about the way we treat those who are different from us? Do you think that the people described in the passage acted in a civilised way towards the wild boy? Discuss and explain your reasons.

The Author's Craft

1. The author often begins paragraphs by giving dates, or using phrases such as 'As time passed'. Why do you think the author chooses to do this?
2. Why does the author frequently give the names of places, people and their roles or positions in society?
3. Does the author give the reader any indication of his attitude to the wild boy, or those who used him for their own purposes?
4. Why does the author introduce the references to Thomas Malthus and his theories? What has this to do with the wild boy?
5. Does the fact that the passage is written in the third person, past tense, affect how the reader responds to the events described?
6. In the final lines, the writer has briefly outlined what happened to the wild boy, after the experiments ended. How did the writer expect the reader to react to this information?

Unit 9

Feral Children

Wild children, who have apparently been nurtured in the wild by animals, have cropped up throughout history. The Roman Empire was reputed to have been founded by Romulus and Remus, who had been raised by wolves. Feral children include those who, by some twist of fate, have been raised in a non-human environment, and because of it did not learn how to communicate or behave in a human manner.

Case Study A

Name:	Kaspar Hauser
Location:	Nuremburg
Date of referral:	1828
Age:	Approximately 16
Appearance:	Peasant clothing. Dark double-breasted jacket, smock shirt, breeches, boots in poor repair.
Health:	Good. Feet seem unusually soft. Seems unable to use his fingers properly.
Characteristics:	Innocent smile. Indistinct speech might give an impression of being drunk or dumb. Constantly repeats, "Ein Reiter will ich werden, wie mein Vater einer war" (I want to be a rider like my father).
Comment:	Carried a letter to the Captain of the 4th squadron of the 6th cavalry regiment.
Destination:	Found murdered 1833

http://www.occultopedia.com/f/feral_children.htm

Case Studies/Biography Unit 9

Case Study B

Names:	Kamala and Amala
Location:	Found with wolf cubs, in an abandoned termite mound, India
Date of referral:	1920
Source of referral:	Reverend J.A.L. Singh
Age:	Kamala approximately 7-8 Amala approximately 1-2
Appearance:	Naked
Health:	Calloused knees and palms. Sharp-edged teeth. Acute senses of smell, hearing and sight.
Characteristics:	Ferocious. Unable to play with other children. Preferred the company of cats and dogs. Nocturnal. Enjoyed eating raw meat. Walked on all fours. No language.
Comment:	Developed worms, diarrhoea and dysentery 1921.
Destination:	Amala died of illnesses 1921. Kamala would not leave coffin. Kamala suffered a repeat of the same illness and died 1929.

http://www.occultopedia.com/f/feral_children/htm

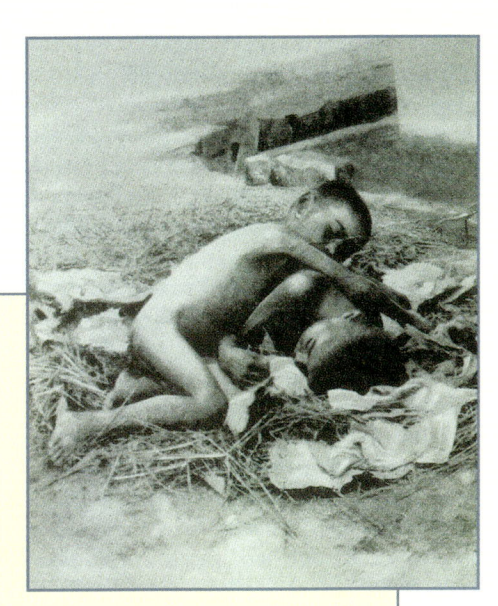

Unit 9 Feral Children

Word Work

1 Explain the meaning of the following words as they are used in the case studies:

Introduction	Case Study A	Case Study B
a feral	d location	h source
b reputed	e referral	i ferocious
c environment	f characteristics	
	g destination	

2 Find expressions in the passage which mean:
   a a shirt-like outer garment, worn by peasants, with the upper part gathered into folds
   b a large, permanent unit of the army, divided into further small units
   c active at night
   d an ant-like, tropical insect, destructive to timber

What is the passage about?

Case Study A
1 What was the name of the strange boy in the Case Study?
2 When and where was the boy discovered?
3 What did he look like?
4 What phrase did he keep repeating?
5 What was he carrying with him when he was discovered?

Case Study B
6 What were the names of the girls in the case study?
7 Where and when were they found?
8 Who found them?
9 How did the girls behave?
10 What happened to them in the end?

Case Studies/Biography Unit 9

Discussion

> The case studies are examples of **non-fiction writing**. In Case Study A, a mysterious boy has been found, who appears to have been living wild in the forests in Germany. In Case Study B, two small girls have been found living in a wolf's den, in India.

A In your groups, discuss and make notes on the following:
- the impressions that you gain of the feral children
- how the appearance of the feral children differs from 'normal' children
- the behaviour and characteristics of feral children
- how successful feral children are at adapting to living in society
- the similarities and the differences between Case Studies A and B
- what might have been in the letter carried by the boy in Case Study A

B What do you think our attitude to feral children would be today? Do you think that they would be treated any differently? Discuss and explain your reasons.

The Author's Craft

1. Why do you think that the writer chose to present the case studies in table format?
2. What are the advantages and disadvantages of presenting information in a table?
3. What do you notice about the writer's use of sentences in the case studies?
4. What does the way the case studies are presented reveal about the writer's attitudes to their subjects?
5. How do the illustrations affect the reader's reactions to the case studies?
6. At the end of each case study is a category called 'Destination'. Does this seem a suitable heading for what happened to the feral children?

AUSTRALIA

Unit 10

Walkabout

Peter and Mary are two children on their way to visit their Uncle Keith in Adelaide. The small cargo plane they are travelling in crashes, the pilot dies and they are left alone in the Australian desert, fourteen hundred miles from their destination. They begin walking southwards to the sea, stopping only to look for food, when they encounter an Aboriginal boy.

The three children stood looking at each other in the middle of the Australian desert. Motionless as the crops of granite they stared, and stared, and stared. Between them the distance was less than the spread of an outstretched arm, but more than a hundred thousand years.

Brother and sister were products of the highest strata of humanity's evolution. In them the primitive had long ago been swept aside, been submerged by mechanisation, been swamped by scientific development, been nullified by the standardised pattern of the white man's way of life. They had climbed a long way up the ladder of progress; they had climbed so far, in fact, that they had forgotten how their climb had started. Coddled in babyhood, psycho-analysed in childhood, nourished on predigested patent food, provided with continuous push button entertainment, the basic realities of life were something they'd never had to face.

It was very different with the Aboriginal. He knew what reality was. He led a way of life that was already old when Tut-ankh-amen started to build his tomb; a way of life that had been tried and proved before the white-man's continents were even lifted out of the sea. Among the secret water-holes of the Australian desert his people had lived and died, unchanged and unchanging, for twenty thousand years. Their lives were unbelievably simple. They had no homes, no crops, no clothes, no possessions. The few things they had they shared: food and wives; children and laughter; tears and hunger and thirst. They walked from one water-hole to the next; they exhausted one supply of food, then moved on to another. Their lives were utterly uncomplicated because they were devoted to one purpose, dedicated in their entirety to the waging of one battle: the battle with death. Death was their ever-present enemy. He sought them out from every dried-up salt pan, from the flames of every bushfire. He was never far away. Keeping him at bay was the Aboriginals' full-time job: the job they'd been doing for twenty thousand years: the job they were good at.

The desert sun streamed down. The children stared and stared.
Mary had decided not to move. To move would be a sign of weakness. She remembered being told about the man who'd come face to face with a lion, and had stared it out, had caused it to slink discomfited away. That was what she'd do to the black boy; she'd stare at him until he felt the shame of his nakedness and slunk away. She thrust out her chin, and glared.

Modern Fiction from different cultures Unit 10

Peter had decided to take the cue from his sister. Clutching her hand he stood waiting: waiting for something to happen.

The Aboriginal was in no hurry. Time had little value to him. His next meal – the rock wallaby – was assured. Water was near. Tomorrow was also a day. For the moment he was content to examine these strange creatures at his leisure. Their clumsy, lumbering movements intrigued him; their lack of weapons indicated their harmlessness. His eyes moved slowly, methodically from one to another: examining them from head to foot. They were the first white people a member of his tribe had ever seen.

Mary, beginning to resent this scrutiny, intensified her glare. But the bush boy seemed in no way perturbed; his appraisal went methodically on.

After a while Peter started to fidget. The delay was fraying his nerves. He wished someone would do something: wished something would happen. Then, quite involuntarily, he himself started a new train of events. His head began to waggle; his nose tilted skywards; he spluttered and choked; he tried to hold his breath; but all in vain. It had to come. He sneezed.

It was a mighty sneeze for such a little fellow: the release of a series of concatenated explosions, all the more violent for having been dammed back.

To his sister the sneeze was a calamity. She had just been intensifying her stare to the point – she felt sure – of irresistibility, when the spell was shattered. The bush boy's attention shifted from her to Peter.

Frustration warped her sense of justice. She condemned her brother out of court; was turning on him angrily, when a second sneeze, even mightier than the first, shattered the silence of the bush.

Mary raised her eyes to heaven: invoking the gods as witnesses to her despair. But the vehemence of the second sneeze was still tumbling leaves from the humble-bushes, when a new sound made her whirl around. A gust of laughter: melodious laughter; low at first, then becoming louder: unrestrained: disproportionate: uncontrolled.

She looked at the bush boy in amazement. He was doubled up with belly-shaking spasms of mirth.

Peter's incongruous, out-of-proportion sneeze had touched off one of his people's most highly developed traits: a sense of the ridiculous; a sense so keenly felt as to be almost beyond control. The bush boy laughed with complete abandon. He flung himself to the ground. He rolled head-over-heels in unrestrained delight.

His mirth was infectious. It woke in Peter an instant response: a like appreciation of the ludicrous. The guilt that the little boy had started to feel, melted away. At first apologetically, then whole-heartedly, he too started to laugh.

The barrier of twenty thousand years vanished in the twinkling of an eye.

From Walkabout by James Vance Marshall

Unit 10   Walkabout

Word Work

1 Explain the meaning of the following words as they are used in the passage:

Paragraph 2
a strata
b primitive
c nullified
d coddle

Paragraph 5
e discomfited

Paragraph 7
f intrigued

Paragraph 8
g scrutiny

Paragraph 10
h calamity

Paragraph 12
i vehemence
j unrestrained

2 Find expressions in the passage which mean:
 a The two children stood very still.
 b The prospect of dying was something the Aboriginal people lived with daily.
 c Peter did what his sister did.
 d Mary blamed her brother without giving him a chance to explain.

What is the passage about?

1 Where does the meeting take place?
2 What was it that Mary and Peter 'never had to face'?
3 To what was the Aboriginal boy's life devoted?
4 Why did Mary decide not to move?
5 What was Peter waiting for?
6 What did the children's 'lack of weapons' indicate to the Aboriginal boy?
7 What happened to interrupt Mary's stare and the boy's methodical examination?
8 How did Mary react to this interruption?
9 What was the 'new sound' which made Mary 'whirl around'?
10 How did Peter react?

Modern Fiction from different cultures Unit 10

Discussion

> The extract from *Walkabout* is an example of **modern fiction**. In it, the author explores a situation where two vastly **different cultures** meet.

A In your groups, discuss and make notes on the following:
- the impression you have gained of the three characters
- the contrast between Mary and Peter's way of life and that of the Aboriginal boy
- the vocabulary the writer uses to show this contrast
- how the writer builds up the tension of the situation
- the relationship of the three children before and after Peter's sneeze
- the meaning and effectiveness of the last line of the extract

B Do you find the meeting of these three children realistic? Is this what might happen or not? Discuss and explain your reasons.

The Author's Craft

1 What does the writer mean when he says 'Between them the distance was less than the spread of an outstretched arm, but more than a hundred thousand years'.
2 How does the writer give the impression that Mary feels she is superior to the Aboriginal boy?
3 Why, in the present situation, is the Aboriginal boy actually 'superior' to Mary and Peter?
4 For what reasons was the Aboriginal boy 'in no hurry'?
5 Mary experiences several emotions throughout the passage. In your own words explain her changing feelings.
6 Write a paragraph to explain how the writer uses contrast in the passage.

Botham on Lillee

Ian 'Beefy' Botham was one of England's finest all-round cricketers. In his book, Botham's Century, *he writes about a hundred cricketing characters he has played with and against throughout his career. In this extract he is recalling the Australian fast bowler, Denis Lillee (DK).*

My friendship with DK goes back years, but my admiration for the man as a cricketer goes even further. I have always said, and I have never had reason to change my mind, that he was the finest quick bowler I have ever seen. And that is a big statement, when you think of the calibre of contemporaries such as Andy Roberts, Michael Holding, Bob Willis and Joel Garner, or more recently the likes of Malcolm Marshall and Glenn McGrath.

Considering that he had such serious back problems during his career it's astounding that he managed to maintain his almost perfect delivery action but what made him stand out above all the others was his cricketing brain. Whatever kind of wicket he was asked to bowl on, he was able to adapt to it. If it was one of the old Melbourne Cricket Ground wickets where the ball used to keep slow and low, he would produce off-cutters, leg-cutters and changes of pace. But when we got back to his home ground at Perth, where the surfaces have always been quick and bouncy, he knew exactly where to put the ball there with real hostility. He was a thinking bowler, and without wishing to upset too many of my old chums it has to be said that bowling with the brain is quite unusual among pacemen.

In many ways, though, DK was a typical Australian cricketer, particularly among those of his generation. He was hard and tough on the field. In every game he played, whether it was club cricket, interstate or Test match, he didn't give an inch, and he didn't expect an inch. But once the final ball of the day had been delivered he was also the first to go into the opponents' dressing-room to have a glass of wine or a beer and chew the cud.

He did so much for Australian cricket, he brought the crowds to life. Among later generations we were to see the same thing with Merv Hughes, but DK was the first bowler who, when he was running up to the crease,

BEEFY ON LILLEE

Born: 18 July 1949, Subiaco, Perth
Country: Australia
Tests: 70
Wickets: 355
Average: 23.92
Beefy analysis: The complete fast bowler who could adapt to any type of wicket. DK had an aggressive temperament and was never far away from controversy. My type of player.
Beefy moment: Facing Lillee at his prime in Perth in the late seventies.
Do mention: His reign as Australia's leading wicket-taker lasted for 16 years until Shane Warne surpassed him in the summer of 2001.
Don't mention: Premature baldness.

Personal Recount Unit 11

would be accompanied by the Aussie crowds roaring 'Kill, kill, kill'. The partnership with Jeff Thomson in the 1970s was probably the most feared combination of all time. They were formidable. You had Thomson, unorthodox but lightning-fast and effective at one end, and DK, the perfect machine, at the other.

I'll always remember one game against DK in Perth. He steamed in and when I played and missed at the first ball he came running down the wicket with the old medallion around his neck swinging from side to side. He always did the same thing when he'd just beaten the bat. He used to stand there staring at you, wipe his forehead with his finger, flick the sweat on to the floor, kick the earth, and then turn round and walk back to his run up mark.

The next ball exactly the same happened. I played and missed, he followed through again only this time he came another couple of yards down the pitch before flicking away the sweat, kicking at an imaginary ball on the ground and walking back.

After I missed the third ball, he got even closer and when he beat me again with the fourth delivery, he followed through so far that he was standing less than a couple of feet away from me. There was still the same old exasperated wiping of the forehead and flicking of the sweat but this time it was on to my shirt with the words, 'Jesus Christ, Beefy. Do me a favour mate – you hold the bat still and I'll aim at it.' He was an enormous man and a great opponent, which is why I rate my two centuries against him at Headingly and Old Trafford during that unbelievable series of 1981 as undoubtedly the most satisfying of my career.

My lasting memory of DK has to be of that wonderful action. It was the one you would show to every kid who wanted to be a quick bowler. It had everything – control, rhythm and pace, and the ability to produce swing or seam virtually on call.

From Botham's Century *by Ian Botham*

Unit 11 Botham on Lillee

Word Work

1 Find these words in the passage and explain their meaning in context:

   Paragraph 1
   a calibre
   b contemporaries

   Paragraph 2
   c hostility
   d maintain

   Paragraph 4
   e formidable
   f unorthodox

2 Find these expressions in the passage and explain their meaning in context:
   a 'didn't give an inch'
   b 'brought the crowds to life.'
   c 'He steamed in'
   d 'My lasting memory'
   e 'was never far away from controversy.'

What is the passage about?

1 In the first paragraph, how does Botham express his admiration for Lillee as a cricketer?
2 Why does Botham find it 'astounding' that Lillee had such a 'perfect delivery'?
3 What was the difference between the wicket at the Old Melbourne Club and the wicket at Perth?
4 What does Botham think is unusual among 'pacemen'?
5 Which cricketer of a later generation does Botham compare favourably to Lillee?
6 With whom did Lillee form a partnership in the 1970s?
7 What actions did Lillee perform when 'he'd just beaten the bat'?
8 What is Botham's opinion of his two centuries against Lillee at Headingly and Old Trafford?
9 Why would Lillee be the perfect example for 'every kid who wanted to be a quick bowler'?
10 For how long was Lillee Australia's leading wicket-taker?

Personal Recount Unit 11

Discussion

> Each chapter of Botham's book, *Botham's Century*, is both biographical, giving some details about a cricketer, and personal, as he recollects encounters both on and off the field with these sportsmen. As such, Botham includes both **factual information** and his **opinion** when writing about them.

A In your groups, discuss and make notes on the following:
- Botham's opinion of Lillee. Find quotes from the text to support your views.
- examples of factual information
- the writer's use of comparison
- how Lillee was
  - unique among cricketers
  - typical of Australian cricketers
- the writer's intention in including the *Beefy on Lillee* box

B Discuss the impression you have gained of Lillee from Botham's account.

The Author's Craft

1. What do you think is the purpose of the opening paragraph?
2. Explain in your own words the difference in Lillee before and after a match.
3. What impression is the writer trying to create by describing Lillee in these terms:
   a 'the perfect machine'
   b 'an enormous man'
   c 'an aggressive temperament'
4. What incident does Botham recount which shows that Lillee had a sense of humour?
5. Write a paragraph to summarise Botham's opinion of Lillee. Use your own words as far as possible. Include some quotes to support your views.

Unit 12

Great Barrier Reef

Complex of coral reefs, shoals and islets in the Pacific Ocean off the north-eastern coast of Australia. It extends in roughly a northwest-southeast direction for more than 1,250 miles (2,000km), at an offshore distance ranging from 10 to 100 miles (16 to 160 km), and has an area of some 135,000 square miles (350,000 square km). It has been characterised, somewhat inaccurately, as the largest structure ever built by living creatures.

The reef actually consists of some 2,100 individual reefs and some 800 fringing reefs (formed around islands or bordering coastlines). Many are dry or barely awash at low tide; some have islands of coral sand, or cays; others fringe high islands or the mainland coast. In spite of this variety, the reefs share a common origin: each has been formed, over millions of years, from the skeletons and skeletal waste of a mass of living marine organisms. The 'bricks' in the reef framework are formed by the calcareous remains of the tiny creatures known as coral polyps and hydrocorals, while the 'cement' that binds these remains together is formed in large part by coraline algae and bryozoans. The interstices of this framework have been filled in by vast quantities of skeletal waste produced by the pounding of the waves and the depredations of boring organisms.

European exploration of the reef began in 1770, when British explorer Captain James Cook ran his ship aground on it. The work of charting channels and passages through the maze of reefs, begun by Cook, continued during the 19th century. The Great Barrier Reef Expedition of 1928-29 contributed important knowledge about coral physiology and the ecology of the coral reefs. A modern laboratory on Heron Island continues scientific investigations, and several studies have been undertaken in other areas.

The reef has risen on the shallow shelf fringing the Australian continent, in warm waters that have enabled the corals to flourish (they cannot exist where the average temperatures fall below 70°F [21°C]). Borings have established that reefs were growing on the continental shelf as early as the Miocene Epoch (23.7 to 5.3 million years ago). Subsidence of the continental shelf has proceeded, with some reversals, since the early Miocene.

The water environment of the Great Barrier Reef is formed by the surface water layer of the south-western Pacific Ocean. The reef waters show little seasonal variation: surface-water temperature is high, ranging from 70 to 100°F (21 to 38°C). The

Encyclopedia – CD ROM   Unit 12

waters are generally crystal-clear, with submarine features clearly visible at depths of 100 feet (30 metres).

Forms of life include at least 300 species of hard coral as well as anemones, sponges, worms, gastropods, lobsters, crayfish, prawns, crabs, and a great variety of fishes and birds. The most destructive reef animal is the crown-of-thorns starfish (Acanthaster planci), which has reduced the colour and attraction of many of the central reefs by eating much of the living coral. Encrusting red algae Lithothamnion and Porolithon form the fortifying purplish red algae rim that is one of the Great Barrier Reef's most characteristic features, while the green alga Halimeda flourishes almost everywhere. Above the surface, the plant life of the cays is very restricted, consisting of only some 30 to 40 species. Some varieties of mangrove occur in the northern cays.

In addition to its scientific interest, the reef has become increasingly important as a tourist attraction. Growing concern over the preservation of its natural heritage has led to increased controls on such potentially threatening activities such as drilling for petroleum resources. The extensive use of tourist craft and the sustainability of commercial fishing were controversial matters in the late 20th century.

Supervision of the reef is largely the responsibility of the Great Barrier Reef Marine Park (declared in 1975), which encompasses the vast majority of the area. There are also smaller state and national parks. In 1981 the Great Barrier was added to UNESCO's World Heritage List, and the first comprehensive report on the state of the World Heritage area was produced in 1997.

From Encyclopedia Britannica 2001 CD ROM

Unit 12   **Great Barrier Reef**

Word Work

Writing about a specialist subject such as science, geography, medicine etc often requires the use of technical vocabulary and expressions. You must understand these before you can make sense of the text.

1 Use a dictionary and the context of each of the following words to explain their meaning:

Paragraph 2
a skeletal
b organisms
c calcareous
d coraline algae
e bryozoans
f depredations

Paragraph 3
g physiology
h ecology

2 The passage gives a list of life forms found on and around the reef. Use a dictionary to help you understand what each of the following life forms is:
   a anenomes   c worms   e lobsters   g prawns
   b sponges   d gastropods   f crayfish   h crabs

What is the passage about?

1 Where is the Great Barrier Reef?
2 What area does the Great Barrier Reef cover?
3 How have all the individual reefs which make up the Great Barrier Reef been formed?
4 What forms the "bricks" in this structure?
5 When did European exploration of the reef begin?
6 Where does scientific exploration of the reef continue today?
7 What is the surface temperature of the water around the reef?
8 Which is the most destructive reef animal?
9 In what way, other than scientifically, has the reef become 'increasingly important'?
10 Who is responsible for looking after the reef?

Encyclopedia – CD ROM   Unit 12

Discussion

The passage about the Great Barrier Reef comes from an encyclopedia CD ROM and its purpose is to give **factual information**. When viewed on the screen, the coloured words can be clicked on to take you to other related pieces of text.

A In your groups, discuss and make notes on the following:
- the organisation of the text – agree on a word, phrase or short sentence to sum up what each paragraph is about
- examples of the use of statistics
- for what purpose this text could be used
- the use of the present and past tenses
- the use of the passive voice

B In what ways would you find this passage helpful/unhelpful if you needed information on the Great Barrier Reef? Explain your reasons.

The Author's Craft

1. What is the purpose of the passage?
2. Who do you think is the likely audience?
3. How is the information organised?
4. In which paragraph would the writer add more information about:
   a European exploration of the reef
   b the formation of the reef
   c the preservation of the reef
5. Using as many facts as you can from the passage, devise a chart or fact-file presenting notes to help a reader understand:
   a the reef's extent
   b how the reef was formed
   c the life forms on and around it
   d the water environment around it

51

EXTREME SPORTS Unit 13

The Ants at the Olympics

At last year's Jungle Olympics,
The Ants were completely outclassed.
In fact, from an entry of sixty-two teams,
The Ants came their usual last.

5 They didn't win one single medal.
Not that that's a surprise.
The reason was not for lack of trying
But more for their unfortunate size.

10 While the cheetahs won most of the sprinting
And the hippos won putting the shot,
The Ants tried sprinting but couldn't
And tried to put but could not.

It was sad for the Ants cause they're sloggers.
15 They turn out for every event.
With their shorts and bright orange tee-shirts,
Their athletes are proud they are sent.

They came last at the high jump and hurdles,
Which they say they'd have won, but they fell.
20 They came last in the four hundred metres
And last in the swimming as well.

Modern Poetry Unit 13

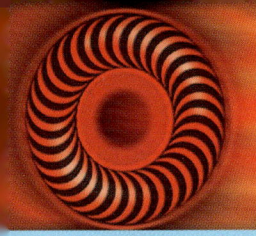

They came last in the long distance running,
Though they say they might have come first.
And they might if the other sixty-one teams
25 Hadn't put in a finishing burst.

But each year they turn up regardless.
They're popular in the parade.
The other teams whistle and cheer them,
Aware of the journey they've made.

30 For the Jungle Olympics in August
They have to set off New Year's Day.
They didn't arrive the year before last.
They set off but went the wrong way.

So long as they try there's a reason.
35 After all it's only a sport.
They'll be back next year to bring up the rear,
And that's an encouraging thought.

From Animal Alphabet *by Richard Digance*

53

Unit 13 The Ants at the Olympics

Word Work

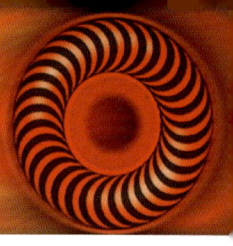

1 Explain the meaning of the following words as they are used in the poem:

Verse 1
a Olympics
b outclassed

Verse 2
c unfortunate

Verse 3
d sprinting

Verse 4
e sloggers
f athletes

Verse 5
g hurdles

Verse 7
h regardless

2 What impressions do the following phrases create in the poem:
   a 'came their usual last.' (v.1, l.4)
   b 'not for lack of trying' (v.2, l.7)
   c 'Though they say they might have come first.' (v.6, l.22)
   d 'So long as they try there's a reason.' (v.9, l.33)

What is the passage about?

1 What impression is created by the use of the word 'usual' in Verse 1, line 4?
2 What impression is created by the use of the phrase 'not that that's a surprise' in Verse 2, line 6?
3 What is meant by 'And tried to put but could not' in Verse 3, line 12?
4 Why do you think that the ants are 'popular in the parade', Verse 7, line 26?
5 What is meant by 'Aware of the journey they've made' in Verse 7, line 28?
6 What is amusing and what is sad about Verse 8?
7 Why does the poet say, 'So long as they try there's a reason' in Verse 9, line 33?
8 What does the poet mean when he says 'After all it's only a sport' in Verse 9, line 34?
9 What impression is given of the character of the ants when the poet says, 'They'll be back next year to bring up the rear' in Verse 9, line 35?
10 Why does the poet find it 'encouraging' in Verse 9, line 36, that the ants will be back next year?

Modern Poetry   Unit 13

💬 Discussion

> The poem, *The Ants at the Olympics*, is an example of **modern fiction**, in the form of a **narrative poem**. The poem is an example of **comic verse**, though it contains a serious point.

A In your groups, discuss and make notes on the following:
- the impressions that you gain of the ants
- the popularity of the ants with other competitors
- the poet's attitude to the ants
- modern attitudes to sport in general and the Olympics in particular
- the Olympic ideals and principles
- sport in schools

B What do you think the reader learns from the ants about the qualities of being a good participant in sport? Do you think that the poem makes its point clearly? Discuss and explain your reasons.

💡 The Author's Craft

1. The poet uses rhyme in the poem. What is the pattern of the rhyme scheme?
2. Do you consider the rhyme scheme to be consistent? In what ways does the rhyme scheme help to support the humour of the poem?
3. By counting the syllables on each line, what do you learn about the rhythms of the poem? What pattern of line lengths can you find?
4. In Verse 4, how does the poet create a sense of sympathy and admiration for the ants?
5. In Verse 4, line 1, the poet emphasises particular sounds? Which sounds are stressed and what effects do they have on the line?
6. In Verse 9, line 36, the poet uses a rhyme in the middle and at the end of the same line. What effect does this have on the poem's conclusion?

55

Unit 14

Skate History: All You Ever Wanted to Know About Wheels... and More

Thanks to Adrenalin Magazine

So I gets a call from Mike at the Adrenalin office in London. "Hey Joey," he says, "What do you know about skateboard wheels?" What do I know about wheels? I'm no scientist, I tell him, but I do know that they've come a long way since the early 1900s when metal roller-skate wheels were first attached to a plank of wood.

Of course, it wasn't until around the fifties that proper skateboards were first produced, but the wheels were still made of steel. I remember riding those babies – they would rattle the money-clip off your Lincoln's and the gold right out of your teeth.

The sixties saw the first skate wave kick off. Steel wheels were replaced with clay wheels, but of course, having as much traction as a rubber sole on ice, people were falling all over the place, slamming and sliding right into a state-wide ban on skateboards: the boys down at City Hall considered them too dangerous.

It was Frank Nasworthy who discovered some experimental roller-skate wheels in a friend's warehouse and consequently created the famous Cadillac wheel: the first ever urethane skateboard wheel.

Formulated in the 1930s in Germany, urethane was perfect for the job, with its good abrasion resistance and high resilience. But despite Cadillacs being a hundred times better than their predecessor, they still had drop-in bearings (16 per wheel) which were far from efficient. Frankie didn't have the financial punch at the time to really take the West Coast by storm.

Unfortunately this is where Richard Novak – owner of a company called Roller Sports – stepped into the picture and bought up all of Creative Urethanes' stock. Creative Urethanes was the company where Nasworthy discovered his urethane solution. Novak's 'Road Rider' wheel was the first to feature precision bearings. It went on to dominate the market, quickly followed by Kryptonics and Sims. The problem with the Cadillacs was that the bearings would pop out of the racers if the wheel was too soft. And everyone, of course, wanted a soft wheel.

The progression of riding styles obviously dictated the type of wheel required. Back then, speed and grip were key, meaning bigger wheels poured in their purest form: i.e., clear or white, with no colour. Any additional colouring would take up more room within the chemical structure of the urethane, meaning less urethane per wheel, which in turn meant a slightly harder wheel with less grip. Sounds complicated, but it's just like making concrete boots – you gotta get the mix right.

Come the eighties, however, and coloured wheels were everywhere. You only have to watch the original Bones Brigade video to see why – we were all power-sliding everywhere, high speed, lay back slides with big gloves on our hands. Take a set of black Slimeballs for instance (a Santa Cruz product, owned by Novak's company, NHS – nice outfit!): you could have a set of 95a wheels and find them as hard and slide-y as a set of pink 98a. Black has more pigment than any other 'colour', taking up much more room in the structure. Capisci?

Unit 14 Skate History

Dropping in on Grandaddy Powell years ago, I recall George was cooking up some chemicals in his kitchen. He was making his first wheels in a homemade mould with a material called 'Upjohn'. The result was amazing. His creations were twice as fast as anything on the market, but he didn't stop there. He discovered that all the other wheels in the industry were made from a Dupont material and started working with both urethanes until he came across the perfect combination of both: exactly 1 to 9. This really is the crux of wheel manufacturing: the raw materials and the process used are far more important to a wheel's performance than its shape and size.

Then came the nineties – Whoa! Wheels became landing gear for skaters who learned to fly, and with this kind of high-impact punishment, they needed to deform less. Engineers refer to the flattening at the bottom of the wheel by a skater's weight as 'deformation'. A resilient urethane wheel returns to its round shape – or 'rebounds' – very quickly. The less resilient a wheel is, the more energy is lost in the deformation, and the wheel will roll away much slower. A harder wheel loses less energy, but if it's too hard, a tarmac road will actually deform and energy will be lost into the road.

More recently, wheels have become harder and smaller in order to suit more technical tricks. Engineers have needed to find a compromise between traction and slide in order to make wheels more forgiving when the board lands at a slight angle – a bit of slide is required. A bulbous, ball-like shape also means landing can be less exact and aids in landing rotational tricks more easily.

So wheels have become harder in order to deal with today's street style, but speed is lost and flatspots wear a lot quicker. This is where dual-durometer comes into play. A durometer is an instrument used to measure a substance's resistance to penetration. The 'A' Shore durometer reads from 0-100, meaning 101a is more of an indication of hardness than an actual measurement. Dual durometer is not a new thing – Nasworthy pioneered that too – but the processes used today are highly technical.

Explanantion Unit 14

To create a wheel with a high abrasion resistance – long life, a high rebound, maintenance of potential energy, and a bearing seat that holds the bearings true – two materials of differing hardness are needed. A hard 'hub' that holds bearings firmly would conventionally use an injection-moulded material. The only problem here is that you can't chemically bond an injection moulded material with the gravity-poured urethane of the 'tyre'. To solve this, engineers created holes or slots in the hard hub that would physically lock together with the gravity-poured urethane 'tyre'.

More innovative companies in recent years have discovered processes that allow them to cast the hub with a gravity-poured urethane – harder than the tyre – which chemically bonds to the softer urethane giving the wheel a more solid feel and eliminating any possible vibrations, translating directly to greater speed. Another problem with injection-moulded hubs is that they will want to reform when subjected to heat, as this is how they are moulded in the first place. Speeding bearings create a great deal of heat, and in a gravity-poured hub there is no softening under heat as the shape is set chemically and not by rapid cooling.

And that's all I know. So if anyone ever refers to your board as a toy, give them a chemistry lesson, and then give Joey Ferreno a call – an' I'll take 'em for a long drive in the desert!

Joey Ferreno

www.withitgirl.com/_skate/historyone.htm

Unit 14 Skate History

Word Work

1 Explain the meaning of the following words as they are used in the passage:

Paragraph 3
a traction

Paragraph 4
b urethane

Paragraph 6
c abrasion
d resilience

Paragraph 8
e capisci

Paragraph 10
f deformation

Paragraph 11
g bulbous

Paragraph 14
h innovative

2 The author uses a number of American expressions. Use the context of the passage to work out what the following mean:
a 'riding those babies' (paragraph 2)
b 'rattle the money-clip off your Lincoln's' (paragraph 2)
c 'Frankie didn't have the financial punch' (paragraph 5)
d 'I'll take 'em for a long drive in the desert!' (paragraph 15)

What is the passage about?

1 When were proper skateboards first produced?
2 When were steel wheels replaced by clay wheels? What were the results?
3 Who created the famous Cadillac wheel?
4 What was special about Novak's "Road Rider" wheel?
5 What did George Grandaddy Powell discover about the raw materials and the processes used to make skateboard wheels?
6 Why did resilience in wheels become important in the nineties?
7 What does a durometer measure?
8 In recent, modern, skateboard wheels, why are two materials of differing hardness needed?
9 Why have recent skateboard wheels become harder and smaller?
10 What are the advantages and disadvantages of injection-moulded and gravity-poured materials for skateboard wheels?

Explanantion Unit 14

Discussion

The passage is an example of **modern, non-fiction writing**, in the form of a **magazine article**. In the passage, a journalist has explained how the technology of skateboard wheels has developed from the 1950s to the present day.

A In your groups, discuss and make notes on the following:
- the impressions that you gain of the development of skateboard wheels
- the contrast between the early attempts to build skateboards and modern approaches
- the technical vocabulary used by the writer to describe the developments in skateboard wheels
- how the writer builds up the relationship between the materials used and the performance of skateboarding
- the use of non-Standard English in writing the article
- the meaning of the final paragraph

B What do you think the reader learns from the magazine article about the technicalities of skateboarding? Do you think that the writer has succeeded in convincing you that a skateboard is not a toy? Discuss and explain your reasons.

The Author's Craft

1 The opening paragraph is not written in full, grammatically correct, Standard English sentences. What effect does this have?
2 The second paragraph also uses non-Standard English expressions that are American idioms. What impression does this create?
3 After the first two paragraphs, the writer uses less idiomatic language or slang. Why do you think the writer does this?
4 Why has the writer included so many trade names and references to individuals who made skateboard wheels? What effect do you think it was intended to produce?
5 Why does the writer make such extensive use of quotation marks or inverted commas, throughout the article? What does this indicate?
6 In the final paragraph, the writer becomes less technical again. Why do you think he chose to do this?

61

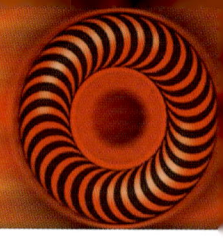

Diving with Sharks

Jack Jackson is a well-known diver and underwater photographer. In this personal recount, he describes some dramatic encounters with sharks.

Six sharks swimming directly towards me, fifty others were counted circling around me, but I forced them out of my mind; hoping that the lure of the bait above my head is stronger than any interest they might have in me personally. The leading shark is one of two large Silvertips 3m long. Swimming up-current its senses are on the dead fish, but its eyes are on me. The strong current slows down the shark's approach, giving me time to focus. One meter away it fills the frame of the 15mm lens. I fire the camera just before it snaps at the bait. Immediately there is an eruption of thrashing sharks, air bubbles, remoras, pilot fish and me, as the snapping action sets off a feeding frenzy. I curse the slow recharge of the flash guns. In thirty-seconds it is all over and I have only managed two more shots.

The sharks quieten down and resume circling. The smaller fish reappear from their hiding places in the coral. I regain my balance, check the cameras and then set myself up for another shot.

Sharks feed infrequently and mostly at night, but will feed opportunistically during the day. They can detect vibration over long distances and are particularly attracted to the vibrations emanating from distressed fish. I have often seen sharks swim into a shoal of fish at high speed and take just one individual fish. Speared or hooked fish struggle violently. In the early 1970s I often dived from fishing boats while their crews were fishing with hook and line. When fish were hooked, sharks would often rocket up from the depths and take the fish off the hook; they showed no interest in divers that were in the water at the time. In the Sudanese Red Sea fishermen can rarely fish in one place for more than fifteen minutes without sharks taking some of their catch. I have seen a shark puncture a Zodiac inflatable when snatching at a hooked fish.

Personal Recount   **Unit 15**

A common misconception is that sharks will not attack in the presence of dolphins. In the late 1980s American underwater photographers discovered that they could attract dolphins' attention for photography by imitating the dolphins' playful behaviour of tumbling and spinning. In June 1990 two of us had been feeding sharks at ShaAb Rumi and when we returned to the surface we found three large Bottlenose Dolphins nearby. My friend swam over to them, turned a few somersaults and was immediately attacked from below by the sharks we had been photographing a few minutes earlier. Our boatman drove off the sharks with the inflatable, but we will never know what caused the attack; the dolphins were larger than the sharks. The sharks may just have been defending their territory, or a diver splashing around on the surface in open water may have appeared to be in trouble, but this emphasised that one should not be on the surface in open water when there are sharks about. If the sharks were defending their territory it was presumably against the dolphins, as they had not given us any problems below.

During shark feeds, the whine of recharging flash guns often elicits an exploratory bite and sharks that normally prey on smaller fish see small light coloured objects as possible prey so never wave your hands about. Several sharks and larger groupers often bite light coloured fins and the glint of sunlight on face-masks, camera lenses and knives may be why these attract close interest. Similarly, medium sized predators are attracted to divers' exhaust bubbles.

On one dive at Sanganebs Southwest Point, two of us were trying to attract sharks with a couple of dead fish on a coral head that we regularly used but this time we were not having any luck. My friend tried cutting the bait into smaller pieces but that still did not have the desired effect.

Unit 15 Diving with Sharks

Eventually, with air running low, he took the bait into the stronger current over the drop-off and shredded it into tiny pieces, that worked too well, he suddenly dropped the lot and headed back to the safety of the reef-wall as a Tiger Shark appeared.

On another occasion at the same coral head, what began as a routine shark feed was to turn nasty. Several divers were positioned around bait attached to chain, which in turn was attached to a security rope. This normally attracted over forty sharks that would circle us, gradually becoming more daring. The stronger the current the farther the scent of the dead fish would carry, attracting more sharks. Eventually one of them would snap at the bait setting off a feeding frenzy.

This dive was different. Only eight sharks appeared, all unusually wary, so I chopped the bait into smaller pieces to release more scent. Suddenly these sharks vanished and out of the gloom came a battle-scarred male Silky Shark, large, fast, sinister and trouble. Swimming at high speed, snapping at each of our heads, the shark kept us busy fending it off, as each diver thumped it on the snout it would hassle another. Finally it snatched the bait.

Few sharks are strong enough to lift heavy chain but this one was. Time stood still while the shark mesmerised us with frenzied twisting and spinning, attempting to free its prize, but when the security rope curled dangerously around a diver I had to cut it free and the shark escaped with its booty. At this stage we felt it wise to carefully retreat to the boat.

The result of any shark encounter depends on your luck on the day but for underwater photographers preparation is 90% of that luck. The old adage: F8 and be there, is vital.

Most people think of the Red Sea as calm, in fact in winter it can get very rough and the gap between waves is generally so short that most boats cannot ride the waves but while descending one are crashing into the next.

Personal Recount **Unit 15**

From the late 1970s till late 1986 I used a fast twin-engined 12m boat and would normally take 2 hours to get from Port Sudan to Sanganeb. I had some very rough journeys that were much more scary than anything that I experienced when climbing in the Himalayas, even on the 8000m South Face of Annapurna. At one time I made several attempts to get to Sanganeb over three days but it was too rough and I had to keep turning back and shelter behind Wingate Reefs. I drove the boat from its flying bridge so my head was over 12 foot above the surface, yet, quite often the inflatable that I was towing would be above my head in the swell.

There still is and always will be plenty to write about when it comes to the sea and its inhabitants. I have at least one book in the pipeline and an awful lot of work ahead!

Interview by Peter Collings
From http://www.sportextreme.com/phdiar31/

Unit 15 Diving with Sharks

Word Work

1 Explain the meaning of the following words as they are used in the passage:

Paragraph 1
a lure
b eruption
c frenzy

Paragraph 3
d infrequently
e opportunistically
f emanating

Paragraph 4
g misconception

Paragraph 5
h elicits

Paragraph 9
i mesmerised
j booty

2 Find expressions in the passage which mean:
  a A boat made of plasticised rubber that is made usable by blowing it up with compressed air.
  b The noise of the flash guns causes the sharks to become aggressive.
  c A raised platform on a boat, from which the helmsman can obtain a good view when steering.
  d The writer is currently preparing to write the next book.

What is the passage about?

1 How many sharks were surrounding Jack Jackson in the opening paragraph?
2 How often and when do sharks usually feed, according to Jack Jackson?
3 Jack Jackson names several species of sharks that he encountered. Name three types.
4 In which sea was Jack Jackson diving?
5 How long were Red Sea fishermen able to fish in one spot before sharks took some of their catch?
6 In what month and year was Jack Jackson feeding sharks at ShaAb Rumi?
7 How long did it normally take him to travel from Port Sudan to Sanganeb?
8 He names several things that might cause sharks to attack divers. Find three examples.
9 How do the divers attract sharks to come near enough to photograph?
10 Jack Jackson compares his journeys across the Red Sea in winter with his experience of another frightening expedition. What was it?

Personal Recount Unit 15

Discussion

The passage is an example of **non-fiction**, **personal recount**. In the extract, an experienced diver and underwater photographer describes a series of incidents involving sharks. He explains a great deal about sharks and corrects some of the myths surrounding their behaviour. Jack Jackson's personal recount includes both **factual information** and his own **opinion**.

A In your groups, discuss and make notes on the following:
- examples of factual information
- Jack Jackson's opinions of shark behaviour. Find quotes to support your views.
- Jack Jackson's use of vivid language when describing the actions of the sharks
- how Jack Jackson builds up the tension of the situation, when describing the incident with the Silky Shark
- the relationship between sharks, dolphins and divers
- Jack Jackson's use of technical language, appropriate to underwater photography and diving

B Discuss the impressions you have gained of shark behaviour and the excitements and dangers of photographing them in their natural environment.

The Author's Craft

1 What do you think is the purpose of the opening paragraph?
2 What impression is Jack Jackson trying to create of the behaviour of sharks when he uses these terms:
   a 'its senses are on the dead fish but its eyes are on me'
   b 'sharks would often rocket up from the depths'
   c 'a common misconception is that sharks will not attack in the presence of dolphins'
3 Jackson describes incidents in which the behaviour of divers causes sharks to act aggressively. Find quotes from the text that illustrate these incidents.
4 Why does Jack Jackson give examples of dates, places and measurements?
5 Write a paragraph to explain how this passage has presented swimming with sharks as something you would or would not like to do.

SCHOOL DAYS

Unit 16

Jane Eyre

Jane Eyre, an orphan, is sent to board at the bleak and unwelcoming Lowood School. She has arrived late at night, slept fitfully and awoke to face her first day.

When I again unclosed my eyes, a loud bell was ringing; the girls were up and dressing; day had not yet begun to dawn, and a rushlight or two burnt in the room. I too rose reluctantly; it was bitter cold, and I dressed as well as I could for shivering, and washed when the basin was at liberty, which did not occur soon, as there was but one basin to six girls, on the stands down the middle of the room. Again the bell rang: all formed in file, two and two, and in that order descended the stairs and entered the cold and dimly-lit schoolroom: here prayers were read by Miss Miller; afterwards she called out –
"Form classes!"

A great tumult succeeded for some minutes, during which Miss Miller repeatedly exclaimed, "Silence!" and "Order!" When it subsided, I saw them all drawn up in four semi-circles, before four chairs, placed at the four tables: all held books in their hands, and a great book, like the Bible, lay on each table, before the vacant seat. A pause of some seconds succeeded, filled up by the low vague hum of numbers; Miss Miller walked from class to class, hushing this indefinite sound.

A distant bell tinkled: immediately three ladies entered the room, each walked to a table and took her seat; Miss Miller assumed the fourth vacant chair, which was that nearest the door, and around which the smallest of the children were assembled: to this inferior class I was called, and placed at the bottom of it.

Business now began: the day's collect was repeated, then certain texts of Scripture were said, and to these succeeded a protracted reading of chapters of the Bible, which lasted an hour. By the time that exercise was terminated, day had fully dawned. The indefatigable bell now sounded for the fourth time; the classes were marshalled and marched into another room to breakfast. How glad I was to behold a prospect of getting something to eat! I was now nearly sick from inanition, having taken so little the day before.

The refectory was a great, low-ceilinged, gloomy room; on two long tables smoked basins of something hot, which, however, to my dismay, sent forth an odour far from inviting. I saw a universal manifestation of discontent when the fumes of the repast met the nostrils of those destined to swallow it; from the van of the procession, the tall girls of the first class, rose the whispered words –
"Disgusting! The porridge is burnt again!"

Classic Fiction Unit 16

The next day, Jane is enrolled as a member of the fourth class and begins her lessons. She has made the acquaintance of a girl called Helen Burns and is angry at the way she is treated by one of the teachers.

At first, being little accustomed to learn by heart, the lessons appeared to me both long and difficult: the frequent change from task to task, too, bewildered me; and I was glad when, at about three o'clock in the afternoon, Miss Smith put into my hands a border of muslin two yards long, together with needle, thimble etc., and sent me to sit in a quiet corner of the schoolroom, with directions to hem the same. At that hour most of the others were sewing likewise; but one class still stood round Miss Scratchard's chair reading… It was English history: among the readers, I observed my acquaintance of the veranda; at the commencement of the lesson, her place had been at the top of the class, but for some error of pronunciation or some inattention to stops, she was suddenly sent to the very bottom. Even in that obscure position, Miss Scratchard continued to make her an object of constant notice; she was continually addressing to her such phrases as the following: –

"Burns (such it seems was her name: the girls here were all called by their surnames, as boys are elsewhere), Burns, you are standing on the side of your shoe, turn your toes out immediately." "Burns, you poke your chin out most unpleasantly; draw it in." "Burns, I insist on your holding your head up; I will not have you before me in that attitude," etc., etc…

My attention was now called off by Miss Smith desiring me to hold a skein of thread: while she was winding it she talked to me from time to time, asking whether I had ever been at school before, whether I could mark, stitch, knit etc.; till she dismissed me, I could not pursue my observations on Miss Scratchard's movements. When I returned to my seat, the lady was just delivering an order, of which I did not catch the import but Burns immediately left the class, and going into the small inner room where books were kept, returned in half a minute, carrying in her hand a bundle of twigs tied together at one end. This ominous tool she presented to Miss Scratchard with a respectful curtsey; then she quietly and without being told, unloosed her pinafore, and the teacher instantly and sharply inflicted on her neck a dozen strokes with the bunch of twigs. Not a tear rose to Burns's eye; and while I paused from my sewing, because my fingers quivered at this spectacle with a sentiment of unavailing and impotent anger, not a feature on her pensive face altered its ordinary expression.

"Hardened girl!" exclaimed Miss Scratchard; "nothing can correct you of your slatternly habits; carry the rod away."

Burns obeyed: I looked at her narrowly as she emerged from the book closet; she was just putting back her handkerchief into her pocket, and the trace of a tear glistened on her thin cheek.

From *Jane Eyre* by Charlotte Bronte

Unit 16 Jane Eyre

Word Work

1 Adverbs tell us how, when or where an action is done.
   What impression of the characters and their actions is given by the use of these adverbs?
   a 'I too rose **reluctantly**'
   b 'Miss Miller **repeatedly** exclaimed'
   c 'Burns **immediately** left the class'
   d 'the teacher **instantly** and **sharply** inflicted'
   e 'I looked at her **narrowly**'

2 Adjectives describe nouns.
   What impression is given by the use of these adjectives?
   a '**low**, **vague** hum'
   b 'this **inferior** class'
   c 'a **protracted** reading'
   d 'The **indefatigable** bell'
   e 'This **ominous** tool'

What is the passage about?

1 What details in the first paragraph show the girls were awakened before it was light?
2 Why could Jane not get washed as soon as she got up?
3 What was the first thing to happen when the girls reached the 'cold and dimly-lit school room'?
4 How many classes where there?
5 What was the girls' attitude to breakfast? Why?
6 What two things about the lessons did Jane find bewildering?
7 Why did Jane think that Burns had been sent to the bottom of the class?
8 What did Burns bring from 'the small inner room'?
9 How did Burns react to her punishment in front of Miss Scratchard?
10 How did Jane know that Burns had cried in the 'book closet'?

Classic Fiction — Unit 16

Discussion

> *Jane Eyre* is an example of **classic fiction**. It was written by Charlotte Bronte in 1847 and tells the tale of Jane, an orphan, who spends many years at Lowood School both as pupil and teacher. She then becomes a governess and, after many more hardships, marries Mr. Rochester of Thornfield Hall. When it was published, *Jane Eyre* attracted attention and praise. It was, however, criticised by some who felt that, through the main character of Jane, Charlotte Bronte was making a powerful statement of a woman's claim to be independent.

A In your groups, discuss and make notes on the following:
- the words and phrases used to convey the setting
- what is conveyed about the school through the repeated mention of the bell
- the impression you get of:
  - Jane
  - Burns
  - Miss Smith
  - Miss Scratchard
- your feelings about Burns' punishment and her reaction

B By careful attention to detail list any similarities and differences between your school and Lowood.

The Author's Craft

1. From evidence in the text, what impression do you get of the discipline in the school?
2. In your own words, explain the following:
   a. 'a great tumult'
   b. 'a universal manifestation of discontent'
   c. 'your slatternly habits'
3. How does the narrator portray the different characters of Miss Smith and Miss Scratchard?
4. What impression does the writer convey of Helen Burns?
5. Are there signs in the passage that Jane will rebel against the way things are done at Lowood? What are they?

The Other Side of the Dale

Gervase Phinn worked as an Inspector of Primary schools in Yorkshire. In his book he recounts many humorous incidents. The following extract concerns the five nativity plays he was invited to at the end of one Christmas term!

At the first, I had approached the school to find all the children heading for home. I had stopped a small boy loaded down with Christmas cards, calendars, decorations, presents and all manner of boxes and bags as he tried to negotiate the narrow gate.

'Where's everyone going?' I had asked. 'There's a nativity play here this afternoon, isn't there?'

He had stopped for the amount of time it took to tell me bluntly, 'It's off!'

'It's off?' I had repeated.

'Aye,' he replied. 'T'Virgin Mary's got nits!'

The second nativity play I had seen had not started off all that well. The seven-year-old introducing the Christmas play had announced, after a number of unsuccessful attempts, 'Welcome to our Harvest Festival.' I learnt later that she could not pronounce the word 'nativity'. Things had improved after this initial hiccup until the little girl with the lead part of Mary had begun to find that the thick robe and headdress made her more and more hot and sticky as the play progressed. As the Magi had presented her with their gifts she sighed and thrust the large doll representing the baby Jesus with a fair bit of force onto the lap of Joseph, saying in a loud stage whisper as she did, 'You have him a bit, he's getting heavy.'

At the third nativity play I had overheard a conversation at the side of the stage between two cherubic six-year-olds dressed in white silk trimmed with silver and speckled with sequins. It was an exchange not meant for the audience's ears. One child had remarked, 'I feel a right twit in this, don't you Gavin?' His companion had agreed, nodding vigorously. 'And if she thinks I'm being a flipping snowflake next year she's got another thing coming!'

The little actor in the fourth nativity play I watched had looked very disgruntled. I heard later that the lead part of Joseph had been given to another child and he had not been too pleased. He had argued with his teacher to no avail and had been given the role of the innkeeper. On the night of the performance Mary and Joseph had arrived at the inn and had knocked boldly on the door. The innkeeper, who had remained grumpy all through rehearsals, had opened the door with a great beaming smile. 'Innkeeper, innkeeper,' Joseph had begun, 'we have travelled many miles in the darkness and the cold. May we come in?'

'She can come in,' he had said, pointing to Mary, 'but you can push off!'

I was now about to watch the fifth version of one of the most famous and powerful stories of all time, and wondered what gem might be produced tonight. The curtain opened to reveal the outlines of various Eastern-looking houses painted on a backdrop and two rather forlorn palm trees made out of papier mâché and green crêpe paper which drooped in the centre of the stage. The little boy, playing the lead as Joseph, entered wearing a brightly-coloured towel over his head and held in place by an elastic belt with metal snake fastener. He took centre stage without a trace of nerves, stared at the audience and then beckoned a particularly worried-looking Mary who entered pulling a large cardboard and polystyrene donkey.

'Come on!' urged Joseph. 'Hurry up!' He banged on the door of one of the houses. 'Open up! Open up!' he shouted loudly.

The innkeeper, with a face like a death mask, threw open the door.

'What?' he barked.

'Have you any room?'

'No!'

'You have!'

'I haven't!'

'You have, I saw t'light on.'

'I haven't.'

'Look, we've travelled all night up and down those sand-dunes, through dusty towns, over hills, in and out of rivers. We're fit to drop.'

'Can't help that, there's no room,' replied the innkeeper.

'And I've got a wife out here on t'donkey.' Joseph gestured in the direction of a very glum-looking Mary who was staring at the audience, her face completely expressionless.

The innkeeper remained unmoved. 'And you can't leave the donkey there. You'll have to move it!'

'Well give us a room.'

'There's no room in the inn. How many more times do I have to tell you?'

'She's having a baby, tha knaws.'

'Well, I can't help that, it's nowt to do with me.'

'I know,' replied Joseph sighing as he turned to the audience, 'and it's nowt to do with me neither.'

To the surprise of the children there were great roars of laughter from the audience.

From The Other Side of the Dale *by Gervase Phinn*

Unit 17 The Other Side of the Dale

Word Work

1 Some of the humour in this extract comes from the use of dialect and idioms. Translate the following into Standard English:
  a "Aye… T'Virgin Mary's got nits."
  b "You have him a bit…"
  c "…she's got another thing coming."
  d "…you can push off."
  e "She's having a baby, tha knaws."

2 Find these expressions in the passage and decide which of the meanings fits best.
  a Is the child who is trying 'to negotiate the narrow gate' trying to
    get through it or *argue with it*?
  b Does an 'initial hiccup' mean
    the first hiccuping noise or *something going wrong at the beginning*?
  c If you argue 'to no avail' does it mean
    you argue successfully or *you argue unsuccessfully*?

What is the passage about?

1 Why was the writer surprised as he approached the first school?
2 Why did the seven-year-old at the second nativity play announce, "Welcome to our Harvest Festival"?
3 In your own words explain what Gavin and his friend were talking about at the side of the stage.
4 Why was the 'little actor' in the fourth play so disgruntled?
5 What did he say to Joseph that was obviously not part of the script?
6 Out of what had the scene for the fifth nativity play been made?
7 How was Joseph dressed?
8 How was Joseph's attitude to being on stage different from Mary's?
9 What does Joseph tell the innkeeper to persuade him to let them have a room?
10 Why do you think there were 'great roars of laughter from the audience'?

Autobiography Unit 17

💬 Discussion

> This extract is one of many humorous episodes that Gervase Phinn **recounts** in his book *The Other Side of the Dale*. It is made up of his **personal experiences** during his time as an inspector of primary schools.

A In your groups, discuss and make notes on the following:
- how the structure of the extract builds up the humour
- which features of the text create the humour
- examples of the humour
- who the likely audience would be
- personal opinion as to whether you find it funny or not. Give your reasons.

B Exchange humorous experiences from your primary school days.

💡 The Author's Craft

1 What evidence in the text is there to suggest that the writer:
  a enjoyed his work
  b likes children
2 Explain in your own words:
  a 'It was an exchange not meant for the audience's ears.'
  b 'very disgruntled'
  c 'what gem might be produced'
3 Give at least two examples from the text to show that the writer observed things closely.
4 What impression is created by the verbs in the following:
  a ' "Come on," **urged** Joseph.'
  b ' "What?" he **barked**.'
  c 'and **thrust** the large doll'
5 By the time the writer gets to the fifth nativity play, he wonders what 'gem might be produced'. As the reader, are you expecting everything to go smoothly or not? Explain your reasons.
6 Explain in your own words why the audience found Joseph's last remark so funny.

75

Unit 18

National Testing in Schools – Two opposing arguments

SATs and stress – give us a break!

Three cheers for SATs! Last year's Science scores were up 7% at Key Stage 2, reading was up by 5% and English overall was up by 4%. Without wishing to dampen the glee of teachers, parents and pupils buoyed by their continued success, the figures hide underlying concerns over the validity and usefulness of these results. This was most recently demonstrated in the debacle over the writing tests, with over 5,000 appeals against the recorded writing scores lodged with the QCA in 2000 alone. The National Primary Heads Association has also taken soundings from several schools, and suggests a 40-50% difference between scores for the same pupil in reading and writing tests. Something is clearly wrong.

The controversy surrounding this latest challenge to the authority of the SATs is something teachers have long grown accustomed to. Adding to this debate is the ongoing worry that pupils are being put under unnecessary and unreasonable pressure. Teachers have voiced concerns that SATs may lead to the well-documented situation in Japan, where a spate of child suicides has been attributed to the increasing pressure put on young children to pass exams. Already in the UK this year, more than 1 in 10 of the 780 calls made to Childline about exam stress were from children under 13. However much teachers and the government may play down the importance of the annual tests, it seems that pressure and anxiety are being transmitted to children. Acquiring basic skills is fine, but fostering nervous anxiety in vulnerable 11-year-olds is clearly not.

Parents, publishers and resource providers may also be fuelling this fire, with attractively priced revision packs and crammers for Key Stage 1 and 2 pupils promising instant SAT success. But who does it all benefit in the end? Teachers remain largely sceptical of the notoriously labour-intensive tests. Their only apparent aim is to give a snapshot of pupil performance, yet in reality they are used to establish the reputation of the school, to benchmark teachers' threshold payments, and increasingly, according to some teachers, to give credence to government initiatives such as the Literacy and Numeracy Strategies.

As far as pupil education is concerned, are the SATs largely irrelevant? Is there a better way of monitoring progress, and should teachers give stressed out primary aged children a break?

All site contents copyright © Spark Learning Limited, 2000
Email us at feedback@sparklearning.com

Acknowledgements

The authors and publisher gratefully acknowledge permission to reproduce the following copyright material:

Robert Service, *The Duel*: H.W.M. Krasilovsky, as agent/attorney for the Service Estate.

Michael Parkinson & Clyde Jeavons, *Western Films*: Hamlyn.

Review of Vidal's *Billy the Kid*: Marilynn Milam, www.planetkiller.com.

Shd skools ban txt msgs?: Catherine Minnis.

Peter Charlton, *Wolf Boy*, copyright © Peter Charlton, 1985 (*Learning From Life, Five Plays for Young People*, ed. John Lonie, Currency Press, 1985): Cambridge University Press & Currency Press Pty Ltd.

Wild Boy of Aveyron and *Feral Children*: Marcus V. Gay, www.occultopedia.com.

Walkabout by James Vance Marshall (first published as *The Children* by Michael Joseph, 1959) copyright © James Vance Marshall, 1969: The Penguin Group (UK).

Ian Botham, *Botham's Century*: Reprinted by permission of HarperCollins Publishers Ltd © Ian Botham, 2001.

Great Barrier Reef: Encyclopedia Britannica Inc., Chicago

The Ants at the Olympics (pp. 7-8, 36 lines) from *Animal Alphabet* by Richard Digance (Michael Joseph, 1980) copyright © Richard Digance, 1980: The Penguin Group (UK).

Joey Ferreno, *Skate History*: Rich Beach at Adrenaline Magazine, and withitgirl.

Diving with Sharks: Peter Collings.

The Other Side of the Dale by Gervase Phinn (Michael Joseph, 1988) copyright © Gervase Phinn, 1988: The Penguin Group (UK).

The Campaign for Real Education: Nick Seaton, copyright © 2000-2002 Families.

SATs and Stress – Give us a break!: This article was first published on the Spark Island website at http://www.sparkisland.com and is printed here with the permission of Spark Learning Limited.

Efforts to contact other copyright holders have proved unsuccessful. If any of them would care to contact Badger Publishing, we will be happy to make appropriate arrangements.

Illustrations by:

Page 5   *The Duel* – Ross Watton

Page 28 *Wolf Boy* – Gilly Marklew

Page 33 *The Wild Boy of Aveyron* – Mike Lacey

Pages 52-53 *The Ants at the Olympics* – Nick Diggory

Page 73 *The Other Side of the Dale* – Tania Konstant

The authors and publisher also gratefully acknowledge permission to reproduce the following copyright photographs:

Page 9 – Broncho Billy © Topsham Picturepoint

Page 13 – Val Kilmer as Billy the Kid © Rex Features

Page 16-17 – Pierce Brosnan as Robinson Crusoe/William Takaku as Friday © Moviestore Collection

Page 24-25 – BMW 23/Chrysler PT Cruiser © AutoExpress

Page 36-37 – Kasper Hauser/Amala and Kamala © Mary Evans

Page 45 – Denis Lillee © EMPICS

Page 48 – Great Barrier Reef © Corbis UK Ltd

Page 49 – Great Barrier Reef © TRIP/A. Tovy

Page 56 – Skateboarding © Rex Features

Page 57-58 – Skateboarding © TRIP

Page 59 – Skateboarding © Popperfoto

Page 62-64 – Diving with Sharks © Rex Features

Page 65 – Diving with Sharks © Jonathan Olley/Network

Badger Publishing Limited
26 Wedgwood Way
Pin Green Industrial Estate
Stevenage
Hertfordshire SG1 4QF
Telephone: 01438 356907
Fax: 01438 747015
www.badger-publishing.co.uk
enquiries@badger-publishing.co.uk

Between the Lines Book 2
ISBN 1 85880 885 5

Text © Wendy Wren and Geoff Reilly 2002
Complete work © Badger Publishing Limited 2002

All rights reserved. No part of this publication may be reproduced, stored in any form or by any means mechanical, electronic, recording or otherwise without the prior permission of the publisher.

The right of Wendy Wren and Geoff Reilly to be identified as authors of this Work has been asserted by them in accordance with the Copyright, Designs and Patents Act 1988.

Publisher: David Jamieson
Editor: Paul Martin
Design: Niki Bowers
Design project management: Hilary Davies

Printed in Great Britain

Opinion   Unit 18

Discussion

SATs and Stress – give us a break and *The Campaign for Real Education* are examples of **persuasive articles** where the writers have strong opinions and wish to persuade readers to agree with them.

In your groups, discuss and make notes on the following for each article:
- the writer's viewpoint
- the purpose of the opening paragraph
- the arguments used to support the writer's opinion
- how effective you think the arguments are
- which of the articles you find most persuasive

The Author's Craft

Passage A

1 Given the viewpoint from which the article is written, what is the purpose of the opening sentence?
2 What is the contrast the writer uses in the opening paragraph? Why is this effective?
3 What effect do you think the writer is hoping to have by mentioning suicides in Japan and calls to Childline?
4 Why do you think the writer includes teacher opinion of the SATs?
5 What is the writer implying about the SATs when he says that the 'only apparent aim is to give a snapshot of pupil performance'?

Passage B

6 Why do you think the writer feels it is necessary to begin the article by giving information about the Campaign?
7 Why do you think Nick Seaton's comments would appeal to parents?
8 What do you think he means when he says that the national tests provide 'objective information'?
9 Why do you think the article stresses the important part played by teachers in the testing process?
10 Why do you think he makes a comparison between LEA schools and independent schools?
11 Write a paragraph explaining which of the two articles you find most persuasive.

Unit 18 — National Testing in Schools

Word Work

Use a dictionary and the context to work out the meaning of these words:

1 **Passage A**

   Paragraph 1
   a buoyed
   b validity
   c debacle
   d soundings

   Paragraph 2
   e controversy
   f well-documented
   g fostering

   Paragraph 3
   h sceptical
   i labour-intensive
   j credence

2 **Passage B**

   Paragraph 1
   a ridiculed
   b affiliated

   Paragraph 2
   c assess

   Paragraph 3
   d objective
   e monitor
   f rigorous
   g manipulation

   Paragraph 4
   h indicator
   i attain
   j norm

What are the passages about?

Passage A

1 By what percentage were Science and English scores up at Key Stage 2?
2 In your own words, explain the two underlying concerns about SAT results.
3 What 'ongoing worry' do teachers have regarding pupils and the SATs?
4 What is 'the only apparent aim' of the SATs?
5 Give two examples of what the SATs 'in reality' are used to measure?

Passage B

6 How many adults began the Campaign and in what year?
7 Although Nick Seaton supports SATs, he would like to see improvements. Find two examples of the improvements he suggests.
8 Why are the SATs a 'unique' national test?
9 What must teachers do for each pupil before the test papers are returned?
10 Where has this kind of annual testing been 'the norm'?

The Campaign for Real Education

The Campaign for Real Education is not new (it was started in 1987) but it's worth knowing about and supporting: when the 14 parents and teachers began the Campaign, many of their ideas were ridiculed or branded 'right-wing'. Now however, thanks to their reasoned arguments and use of research evidence, general public opinion has changed in their favour – to such an extent that most of their proposals have been adopted by the Government.

Their aim is to raise standards and improve choice in state education. It is non-profit making and is not affiliated to any political party. They publish a termly newsletter and an ongoing series of pamphlets on important educational issues.

It's SATs Time of Year Again

Parents of primary school children will be now aware of the national curriculum tests which take place in LEA schools each May, at the end of each Key Stage (ages 7, 9 and 11). Created to assess children's progress through school, the national 'league' tables were published in February showing 11 year olds' results in English, Maths and Science, and of course many of us immediately looked up schools we know and made comparisons with the printed figures.

How useful are SATs?

I asked Nick Seaton of the Campaign for Real Education how useful he feels the tables are: "We firmly believe that parents need the objective information provided by national tests, both to see how individual schools perform when choosing a school, and to objectively monitor the progress of their individual child or children. We believe that the administration and costs of national tests should be reduced and the tests should be more rigorous. The 10 level scale is too vague and should be replaced with marks out of 100. The reading ages of all primary pupils should be measured annually by standardised tests (which are available from various sources) and similar tests are needed for arithmetic. The results of all tests for 7, 11 and 14 year-olds should be published locally and nationally by the end of August in the same year as they are taken. Because results from schools in similar areas are sometimes excellent and sometimes very poor depending on the standard of teaching, we do not support the manipulation of test results to show 'value added' results."

So, are SATs useful?

We now have a better indicator of how our children are doing individually, compared to their peers. Also these are unique in being the only national exams where test papers are returned, with some schools inviting parents to see and discuss their own child's marked test papers for themselves. A further benchmark of professionalism is that teachers are required to assess each child and record the level they expect each to attain before test papers are returned. Certainly the whole system adds another layer to an already full day for teaching staff, not only in the administration involved, but whereas annual testing is the norm in independent schools, it hasn't been in LEA schools.

Copyright © 2000-2002 Families